How To Be Free:

A Practical Guide To Positive Living

3

Table of Contents

Introduction

This book is a compilation of ideas I have studied and personally tested for almost a decade in my quest to understand how life works, discover my purpose and learn how to successfully live out that purpose. These ideas are what I know to work. I know this because I have applied them in my own life and have seen amazing results that prove it. Each time I have applied these principles in my life, they have infallibly produced results that match my efforts, so I confidently assert that anyone who applies these ideas in their life will also receive results that are proportional to the consistency of their efforts. I wrote this book to inspire, motivate and empower those seeking to live their higher path and purpose in love, peace, harmony and freedom.

Clearly outlined within this volume are ways to minimize or eliminate negative experiences in one's life by thinking and doing things positively, which increases the degree of success and freedom one experiences. Success and freedom are achieved most easily when one lives in harmony with the laws that govern everything in existence, the laws of nature/creation. It is only through living positively that one can experience life the way it was intended; being free to do, have or become anything one wants to be (that adds to life of course). The keys conveniently put together for the reader in this book are what enabled all great men and women, past and present, to attain the extraordinary success in their lives.

The ultimate goal of life is for intelligent motion to exist and grow perpetually as a result of forever expanding awareness. We all yearn constantly to be able to do, have or be anything we want without any restraints. This reality we seek is what we simply call FREEDOM. The fact that we have these yearnings means we inherently have the ability to satisfy them. Freedom in essence is our ability to successfully accomplish a given idea, so when we discuss freedom we are also discussing success and vice versa. The amount of freedom we experience in any given area of our life is an exact measure of the success we are experiencing in that area.

This book will also outline and further explain in simple terms what freedom is, how to achieve it and promote it by living positively. When one has power to be free in his/her thoughts, one is then able to produce and promote freedom outside of him/her. The unique feature of this writing is the proper identification of the root cause of friction in Life, negative, how it operates and how to avoid it in our thinking. This understanding of the existence of the positive and negative forces in life and how to utilize factual thinking to enable one to make choices that only promote the positive force is the formula for success and freedom. I have used scientific, mathematical, biblical and metaphysical terms to paint a clear picture that answers the why of everything in life, as a way to explain this formula. In addition to that, we shall discuss some common erroneous thought patterns that promote failure and how to replace them with positive thoughts. We will also explore other aspects of life that need to be viewed properly for success and freedom to be part of our reality and how to adjust our thinking and behavior to make ourselves financially free and enable us to live the life of our dreams.

The formula to the attainment of freedom outlined in these pages applies to all entities, from individuals all the way to nations, as a nation is simply a system set up to promote the nature of the people who designed it. When a man is free in his thinking, the nation he sets up will also reflect freedom.

Since a family is the basic unit that represents the motion of a nation, what a man does in his home as a family directly determines what will happen with him as a Nation. A free mind will produce a free home which in turn manifests a free nation.

This book is divided into three chapters that represent the three levels of existence which encompass all Life; spiritual, mental and physical. Chapter 1 defines and then explores the origin and purpose of freedom in life. Chapter 2 discusses how we are to think in order to stay positive and achieve freedom while Chapter 3 outlines and explains what we have to do to become free.

The concepts in this volume require us to have an open mind, a willingness to faithfully apply these ideas to our individual selves and the patience to allow ourselves to grow into the free human beings we were designed to be. As you go through this book, keep this advice in mind; ALWAYS look to PROVE what is being shared as ACCURATE or FACTUAL. It is best to avoid the common tendency to reject or dismiss any ideas that do not fit or agree with what we think we already know. We also have to remember that if what we already know could produce freedom; most of us would already be free, cancelling out the need to even have freedom as a topic of discussion.

Careful study of this small writing will prove to be a very worthwhile investment of your time and energy. Your successful and free future self will surely thank you for it. Some study hints that have worked for me in my life of constant study and growth are; After reading a new concept, take time to reflect on it by seeing how it applies in YOUR own life and experiences. Then write your understanding of the concepts in your own words and most importantly, explain it to somebody else. Have fun!

Being Positive is the Only Way to Success and FREEDOM!

Chapter 1 – The Spiritual

1. Defining Freedom

The concept of FREEDOM is one we can discuss endlessly, especially because of how it is so misunderstood by most. The majority of the population is operating under the illusion that being able to make choices, regardless of the consequences of the choice, is freedom. If you make a choice and as a result of that choice you end up confined to your death bed, can you truly say you are free? Most people think that they already know and understand what freedom is. Do they really? What is freedom? Are YOU free? Free from what or free to do what? If you are not, then why are you not free? Do YOU want to be free? If so WHY and if not WHY not? Is freedom something that somebody has to grant you or can you attain it yourself? How is freedom achieved? These are all crucial questions, which when properly answered will bring much clarity on this important subject.

To set a base, we are going to discuss the levels of existence in a nutshell and then relate them to freedom. Everything exists on three levels, spiritual, mental and physical. This is the trinity, the three in one. There is the WHY or thought behind a thing, then the HOW or intelligence to produce the thought, and finally the WHAT or physical result of the thought. Everything is energy and energy is the force behind motion. Motion is movement or unending expression of activity. Thought is energy directed. An idea is a collection of thoughts aimed towards one purpose. Again, all that exists starts as a thought, which is the purpose, or WHY behind a thing and it is unseen. Then intelligence is gathered as facts on HOW to manifest the thought. When everything needed to produce the thought in its fullness has been put together then we have the physical result of the thought, the WHAT. This is the process all thoughts go through before they manifest physically as everything we see, touch, smell, taste and hear in our physical world. Everything is a representation of a thought that is unseen. Everything around you right now is a manifestation of a thought that started in someone's mind. This is the base that has to be understood for anything in life to make sense. Volumes upon volumes can be and has been written on the few yet profound truths mentioned in this single paragraph.

Science has proven many times over that everything is energy. Everything in the physical world is made up of atoms, and atoms are energy vibrating at different rates to produce matter. Atoms make up solids, liquids and gases; the only difference in these three states of matter is the rate of vibration of the energy within the atoms. The same energy that makes up thought is the same energy that atoms consist of. These same atoms then form solids, liquids and gases. Thought is energy at a very high rate of vibration while solid matter is energy that has slowed down to its lowest rate of vibration. Everything that exists is an expression of energy vibrating at rates between those of thought and solid matter. We cannot see thoughts until they take form as physical things. That is the unseen or spiritual realm manifesting in the seen or physical realm after intelligence has been gathered and applied in the mental realm.

Let us take for example a car. The purpose, the idea behind, or the why of a car is transportation, that is the spiritual aspect of all vehicles, to transport something or someone from point A to point B. This idea started in someone's mind and we could not see the idea physically. Then the idea moved to the mental where facts on HOW to manifest the car were gathered and added up as the blueprints on paper with all the systems and choices of materials. Then everything was put together according to the intelligence gathered to produce the physical car that we can see, touch and drive, which is the WHAT. Now when we look at the car, we are looking at the fullness of the idea that was once unseen. This is an expression of the trinity, the spiritual, mental and physical, the three in one.

Our physical bodies have minds that enable us to think and express our thoughts through what we say, do and produce. As we have heard this many times, we are what we think, because what we think determines everything we say, do and produce which in turn become our life experiences. So the freedom that we seek has to exist on all three levels, spiritual, mental and physical.

A. What is Freedom?
The keyword in freedom is free. What does it mean to be free? We cannot be something we don't know and understand. To be truly free we first have to know what it means and then understand the process of HOW to become free. To be truly free, it has to start in our thinking. One cannot be free in their outside world without being free in their inner world, in their thinking. A lot of wars and battles have been and are being fought in the name of freedom, even though most of those fighting can neither identify nor understand what freedom really is and how to attain it. With the right understanding one will realize it is futile to attempt attaining freedom outside before it is attained within, in one's thinking.

Free is an experience of being able to DO, HAVE or BE something without opposition or hindrance. When one is able to express a given idea and experience it without hindrance then one is free in that respect. For example being free to love, free to move around, free to express oneself etc. What we want most is being free to be ourselves, to express the ideas that make up who we are, to live life the way nature intended. This very idea is of utmost importance as it determines how we will live and experience life. How does one know oneself? How was Life intended to be lived anyway? One has to know who and what they are by nature in order to be able to properly express themselves freely. To know thyself is to know the laws that govern thought and motion within us, and to express ourselves is to express the thoughts and ideas in our minds that bring us joy and that we feel inspired and compelled to share freely with the world.

Freedom is a reality that is void of negative influences. Negative influences produce friction in an idea or motion. When one is able to have an experience, regardless to what they are doing, that has no opposition or friction to it, they are experiencing freedom. Friction retards motion or growth and is a product of opposing forces. In life friction is a result of negative opposing positive, wrong opposing right, falsehood opposing truth, disease opposing health etc.

Everything is energy, even us, therefore the condition of energy being able to have aim, purpose and direction and subsequently achieving that aim and purpose; continuing to grow perpetually with no opposition or restriction is freedom. Our thoughts are energy with aim, purpose and direction. Being able to fully express and manifest our thoughts without experiencing any hindrance is being free. Negative is what hinders us. It is only successful at hindering us because we are not fully aware of its existence and operation within us. The greatest expression of freedom is one of being able to be who we truly are, by manifesting the ideas in us that benefit all life and continuing to grow and develop in our awareness perpetually.

By design we are healthy, intelligent, creative, loving, happy and prosperous beings, among other positive things. The ability to actually be that equates to being free. It takes awareness of what works and applying that awareness to become free. The blueprint of what works is all around us, we call it NATURE. Thinking and conducting ourselves in harmony with the laws of the universe (nature) makes us free. It frees us from the negative experiences that taint our view of life and retard our growth. Remember the old saying, KNOW THE TRUTH and IT SHALL SET YOU FREE? Truth is WHAT IS, or the pattern of life, or nature, and living by this pattern removes us from the bondage of the negative force, the force which is opposed to life and the cause of all limitations and disagreeable conditions in life. Truth is simply the thoughts and ways of the Creator. As evidenced by the mathematical precision of all systems and cycles in the universe, from the galactic and planetary rotations, the cycles that keep everything on the planet working in a balanced way, to even our own body systems, we can see how precise and harmonious the thoughts and ways of the Creator are. When we study, adopt and apply these thoughts and ways of the Architect of Life in our own life, we will attain freedom with mathematical accuracy.

The greatest demonstration of freedom is in our ability to express our purpose in life without restriction. This is what all life yearns for due to the fact that everything wants to be what it was brought into existence for. Wild animals want to be in their wild natural habitat fulfilling their purpose, be it trimming the trees like giraffes, manicuring the grass like cattle and buffaloes, regulating the population of another species like lions and sharks, cleaning up waste like pigs, catfish, shrimps, vultures etc. It is beyond doubt that any animal is happy being confined to a cage or in a zoo because of how so many of their functions are underutilized

16

in that unnatural environment. So it is with us. When we are expressing our purpose, we are most happy, productive and free. We all look forward to a time when we are able to do what we are inspired to do in a way that is in harmony with and which adds to all that exists. In this reality everything supports what we are doing or looking to achieve and even after achieving it, there is no power to bring it back to nothing, only forward moving perpetual growth.

This constant longing to be free is expressed through our love for or fear of something. We love what we think will make and/or keep us free and we fear that which we think will take away or stop us from being free. Free from what? Free from experiencing life's negative expressions. For example, the decisions we make on a day to day basis, they are rooted in our constant want to experience freedom. For instance, one wants a cup of coffee in the morning so that one may stay awake and alert, freeing them from sleep, or eating something so that one is free from hunger, or having a partner, companion or spouse so that one is free from loneliness. We all want to live a life that is filled with pleasurable experiences. Even when we do wrong to produce pleasure, like smoking cigarettes, we temporarily feel good, free from other discomforts like stress, however in the long-term a myriad of health issues will take away our freedom to perform physically. So our lack of understanding of what freedom is leads us to oftentimes look for it the wrong way and or in the wrong places. The place where freedom begins at is in the thinking. As a man thinks, so is he. When one is capable of free thought, one is also capable of attaining and experiencing freedom in all other aspects and expressions of his/her life.

B. Why We Are Not Free

Freedom is a topic of discussion because of the presence of negative, a reactionary force, resulting from creation. Without negative all ideas and motion generated by the positive force will automatically be frictionless and perpetual. The concept of freedom would be non-existent if there was no friction or opposition in the equation of life. To understand this reality we have to explore the origin of the intelligent motion we call life and the forces at play, positive and negative, and their relationship to our quest for freedom.

Positive is the initiating force that started the intelligent motion we now call Creation or Life. This creative force was born out of the want of the energy to be something independent of the nothing and to exist perpetually as intelligent motion. Want is a condition of energy seeking purpose and direction. Nothing is a condition of energy with no aim, purpose or direction. Without intelligent motion, there is no thing with purpose or direction to be counted as something, therefore no creation. When positive went into motion to create something out of the energy that was doing and being nothing, the energy and matter reacted to this motion producing the force known now as negative which manifests in life in expressions that are opposite of or a drag to intelligent motion. As intelligent beings with creative abilities, this process is constantly taking place within us as we develop wants and then conceive thoughts in our minds to satisfy these wants. This is followed by reactions from the negative. Say you have been sitting at home for a long time doing nothing productive and then a want to do something else comes up and you get an idea to go for a walk or drive. That is an example of the positive creative force in us which goes into motion first and is usually automatically followed by a negative reaction. Usually the negative reaction will be a suggestion in our own head in our own voice whispering to us to do something else contrary to positive.

Positive is the producer of right thoughts or ideas that manifest as life's positive attributes like love, compassion, harmony, happiness, intelligence, health, peace, freedom etc. Negative is the reactionary force in Creation that is the generator of all chaotic conditions in existence that are aimed at putting a drag on and eventually stopping intelligent motion or life. It is the producer of wrong thoughts or ideas that are expressed as hate, selfishness, greed, foolishness, disappointment, despair, disease, war, death etc. Negative is always reacting to positive, to cancel out intelligent motion, which is Creation or Life.

The purpose of negative thoughts is to bring positive thoughts back to nothing. This process of opposing thoughts happens to and in all of us as we all have these two forces or natures, positive and negative, in us. We sometimes experience moments of inspiration to do something positive or productive, and then that positive thought is followed by a negative thought of fear that we cannot do it or to do something else contrary to progress. An example is when one is inspired to clean his surroundings, say his place of dwelling. Usually another thought then follows in the form of an excuse why cleaning the house cannot happen right away because it is going to take too long, or one gets a thought to do something else totally different that is non-productive, like smoking a cigarette or playing a video game etc. Another classic example is when one plans to wake up early in the morning to have a productive day, and when the alarm goes off, instead of getting up one presses the snooze button to stay in bed a little longer, cancelling out the initial idea to get up early. In all these examples, negative is attempting to cancel out the positive ideas.

It takes diligence and self-discipline to be right or positive and productive, because this negative force in each of us does not tire from its relentless attempt to stop all positive ideas and motion. This book is intended to equip YOU, the reader, with enough inspiration and guidance to be disciplined enough to constantly practice thinking and doing right in order to experience real freedom first hand and then perpetuate it.

In essence, all we see occurring in life is a constant struggle between Positive and Negative in the form of Truth vs. Falsehood, Honesty vs. Deception, Health vs. Disease, Life vs. Death etc. An illustration of these two forces in us is given in various scriptures and ancient writings or teachings. The most popular teaching is the one about everyone having two angels within, one good and the other evil. Both speak to us constantly and we have to be mindful which one we listen to and obey. One will guide us towards Life while the other towards death. Another Native Indian teaching describes everyone as having two wolves inside. One constructive and the other destructive, and we have to be mindful which one we feed by the type of thoughts we entertain and execute because the one we feed the most will become us.

All thoughts we have are from either of these forces, positive or negative. There is no in-between force or reality. In other words, we are either being positive or negative, and each expression carries automatic rewards or penalties. Since freedom is the goal, this can only be a possibility when we are being positive or right in our thoughts and deeds. Ultimate freedom is attained by ridding one's thoughts and motion of this negative force and all of its effects.

2. The Illusion of Freedom

As mentioned before, the majority of the population on the planet is operating under an illusion of freedom. We think we are free yet we have nothing to show or prove that we are indeed free. This misconception of freedom was programmed into us from our childhood, schooling and through mass media. We think we are free because we believe we have free choice. What we fail to realize is that for the most part what we think are our own choices are choices already made for us by somebody else, those who control our beliefs and opinions. To illustrate this point, say I bring you two apples and ask you to choose which one you like. Have I given you a choice or did I take away your power to choose when I chose which apples to bring to you? This gives the illusion of choice unaware that I already made the choice for you when I picked out which apples to bring to you. The same is true with the things we choose to eat and wear, drive, watch on TV, listen to on the radio, how we look and think about ourselves and the world around us. These are mostly ideas programmed into us by other people through mass media.

What we think are our own thoughts and opinions are in fact thoughts and opinions coming from other people. It is a known fact that if something is continually repeated to you, you will eventually start to believe it, whether it is true or not. TV and movies program us to think that cool people speak, eat, dress and live a certain way by the lifestyles they portray on screen, and now we have millions of people, faithful followers, trying to speak, dress, eat and live a certain way because they have been trained to think it is the acceptable way. It is the people behind the TV telling us how to think and live, so we have no choice in the matter. The ideas that mass media is pumping into our minds, for the most part are not designed to have us experience a life free of error, resistance, pain, disease etc. This scenario makes freedom unattainable. However for most of us, we still think we are free because we get to express our thoughts even though we did not originate them nor are the results of those thoughts in our favor. These programmed thoughts produce friction in our lives because they are not in harmony with the laws that govern our being and everything else, thereby taking away our freedom.

Freedom is produced from the application of truth. When one lives in a world where wrong is the norm and the practice of truth or right is shunned, it is challenging for one to experience freedom. One will have to be taught right/truth and how to apply it in a way that is always in harmony with the laws of nature in order to avoid experiencing friction.

One may circumvent man-made rules and experience freedom; however one may not transgress the laws of nature and be free because of the inevitable built-in consequences. Everyone and everything is subject to laws of nature. The first law of nature is self-preservation. Rules that oppose laws of nature should be broken, because they take away our freedom to live life fully and they will eventually bring one to their death. Breaking rules in order to align oneself with the laws of nature is a matter of self-preservation. Failure to live in harmony with the unbreakable laws of creation/life brings about one's death at a rate directly proportional to the magnitude of their transgression.

Law is that which is set according to the design of life or nature, while a rule is an agreed upon way of doing things in a society in order to govern the motion of the people in that society. Laws can only be transgressed, while rules can be broken and changed as people see fit. Tyrants, oppressors etc. expect other men to transgress laws of nature and obey their rules. Most, if not all of these rules are meant to keep these corrupt individuals in power and in control of others. The cause of most wars is disobedience by people fighting to live life according to nature while others are trying to silence dissent and force others to live under rules that serve only a few corrupt individuals.

If all men strived to put their thoughts and actions in harmony with laws of nature or truth, then we will all experience a higher degree of freedom. Even the ones who oppress and exploit others are not free though they may delude themselves to think that they are. What they have to do to maintain control and the emotions they deal with because of their actions are not conducive to freedom. All the tension, struggle, paranoia, fear, guilt, shame etc. wears them down and soon causes disease and eventually their death.

These corrupt individuals who parade themselves as the powerful are indeed the weakest of our species. When one willingly does something that goes against life and peace, they have surrendered their power to the negative force and are now a willing slave to it. This is a show of weakness by one's lack of self-discipline and self-control, so much so they give up their power to a force that is blatantly against their very existence. Real strength and power is being able to stay positive in thoughts and motion regardless of circumstances in order to promote life and freedom for all.

As long as one is not living according to the laws of nature or truth, freedom will forever be an unattainable reality. Most are deluding themselves that they are free because they are able to do whatever they want to do regardless of the consequences. They are unaware that the negative results from wrong thinking rob them of their freedom to live life fully.

Personal Experiences

I remember vividly growing up thinking to myself, "why is there such a big gap in terms of wealth between people who seem to have the same capabilities?" I had an inherent knowing that something was out of place with the reality I was viewing. More people lived in poverty than those who were wealthy. The wealthy minority controlled the poor majority. I constantly pondered in my own head WHY this was so, though I could not verbalize it to anyone until later on in life. I wanted everyone to have equal share of all the riches because I knew somehow no one person was greater than another. At least I did not view myself as being greater than anyone else. I wanted to be able to do what I want when I want without being restricted by resources. This urge drove me to excel in school because we were taught to think that in order to excel in life one has to excel in school. With all the excellent grades, things were still not making sense to me. I longed to know how things could be setup so that everyone is comfortable, instead of the extremes of wealth and poverty that was common in society. What I was noticing is that there are a few people who seem to have the means to do, have and become anything they want and the majority were not able to. I was one of the disadvantaged majority. I decided later in life, after finding out that those around me did not have the answers I was looking for, to devote my time to finding the meaning of life, and WHY things were the way they were. I also committed to learning what steps where needed to produce a truly peaceful world where everyone is successful and free. My search for the meaning of life, was my yearning to be free from ignorance.

This quest brought me to understand things about life, its origins and purpose and how everything else in life fits in. This clarity has freed me from ignorance and fear and given a peace of mind I would not have gotten otherwise. Understanding the meaning of life, and the forces behind everything we see in the world has given me so much control over my life experiences, leaving me free to determine what type of life I want to live. When I pay attention to the thoughts I have, I can tell when a thought is constructive or destructive just by how it makes my whole body feel. For me, when the feeling is warm and light, it is a positive thought and the negative produces a heavy uncomfortable feeling. Even as I speak to others, I can easily tell, when I am paying attention, whether I am dialoging with the positive side of the person or not. It was later in my studies when I gained a clear understanding of what the relationship between freedom and life was and how everything we learn that makes us better also gives us more freedom. My search and the awareness I gained are evidence of the law of cause and effect at play. I gained understanding through hands-on experience what the great teachers of the past meant by seek and you shall find, ask and you shall be given. I decided to search for the justice that governed the universe, and I found it, and my understanding of it keeps deepening as I continue to relate myself to the same ideas I am sharing with the world in this book. My constant yearning for growth, change and development, fuels me to keep studying, applying, experimenting and I therefore continue growing in awareness. This expansion of consciousness necessitates that I share my new awareness with others so that we can grow together, which frees me from loneliness.

I have operated under the illusion of freedom for a greater part of my life than I have operated in the reality of it. An example of such a misconception of freedom, is when I grew up thinking rules my parents set for us to abide by at home was bondage and very restricting. I later learned in hind-sight that the rules were there for my freedom, to free me from the negative results that living irresponsibly will produce.

Chapter 2 – The Mental

1. How to Attain Freedom

Now that we understand that freedom is a reality derived from a motion or experience which is absent of friction and originates in the thinking, how then does one attain freedom? Simply put, one attains freedom by thinking and doing right. So, what is right? In the following sections we are going to discuss this idea in depth.

A. What is Right?

This is a question that most of us have never really given serious thought to. We assume that the answer is so obvious that asking the question is a waste of time. The ability to discern Right is paramount as it forms the base for us to judge, assess and ascertain everything else in life accurately, or the way things really are by design. Wars, battles, arguments, quarrels, debates and all manner of chaos and confusion are results of not knowing, misunderstanding or downright disregard of what is right. Most people have made themselves to believe that there is no absolute right or wrong. Others prefer not to think and speak in those terms as they believe it amounts to judging. Well, we are always judging, whether knowingly or unknowingly. One cannot make a decision or reach a conclusion without gathering facts, adding them up and then coming to some type of judgment. Identifying 1+1=3 as an inaccurate statement because we know and can prove that 1+1=2 is a form of judgment. Since there is one Source or Creator to everything with set ways of doing and manifesting reality, then that is the obvious guideline or base for us to determine what is appropriate, acceptable, accurate, agreeable or RIGHT in life.

Right is that which can be proven with facts, is in agreement with Nature, and promotes Life and Peace. Nature is the design of a thing, the purpose behind it. The nature of a car is transportation and when we treat and do things that are in harmony with the purpose or nature of a vehicle, we are being right. Life is intelligent motion. When we conduct ourselves in a manner that promotes intelligent motion, we are being right. Peace is the pure expression of mathematics or truth. When all things are expressing their purpose and are being regarded and governed accordingly, then peace is realized. When we allow things or people to express their purpose without interference, then we are being right, as this produces peace.

Thinking right is when the thoughts and ideas we entertain and explore are factual and in harmony with Nature and Life. With the understanding that everything starts as a thought, we are going to spend a great deal of time exploring thought and its processes. When we grasp these thought processes, it will be easier to grasp what is outside that was produced by thought.

Thinking, like any other skill, has to be learned and then practiced for us to become proficient at it. Do you remember how you learned and mastered addition and multiplication tables? It was through practice. Thinking is the gathering and adding up of facts in order to direct energy or matter. There are only two types of thinking, Right and Wrong thinking. Right thinking is the gathering and adding up of facts that produces answers, decisions or conclusions that are in harmony with Nature and promote Life and Peace. Anything else is wrong. Right is synonymous with Positive though in reality positive is the base of what is right.

To be right, we have to be in complete compliance with the laws that govern thought and motion, laws of nature/creation. This equates to being in sync with the positive force. This way we flow with the intelligent motion of the universe, making us free to accomplish any and all ideas that are in harmony with the rest of Creation. All our ideas and motion that are in agreement with life are supported by the power that governs the overall intelligent motion of the universe. This means our motion seamlessly blends in and grows naturally within this universal order. This is freedom as there is no friction, no opposition, and no hindrance.

Since negative is a reaction to positive, it has no power over positive except for the power that we, intelligent beings, give it by doing or carrying out the negative or wrong thoughts it suggests to us. In other words, a reaction is predictable therefore can be avoided or contained. This means we can ensure negative does not disrupt our intelligent motion. When we grasp the laws that govern thought and motion, we are able to formulate plans that can be carried out flawlessly, by being impervious or immune to negative influences. We can do this with our own thoughts, our motion and our interactions with everyone and everything else.

The more we know about a particular idea or thing, the more prepared we are to interact with it harmoniously. The more we know about the purpose of someone or something, the more freedom we will experience in our interaction as long as we put ourselves in harmony with that purpose. For example, the more Truth we know about our bodies in terms of functions and how to treat them right, the more capable we are to use them intelligently and efficiently, therefore having our bodies serve us better, longer, and without issues. The more things, ideas, situations and people that we know the truth about and then apply that truth in our interactions, the more freedom we will experience. The amount of truth or right one applies in their thoughts and motion equals the degree of freedom one experiences. The degree of freedom one experiences is determined by the level of success one achieves in their thoughts and motion, therefore Success equals Freedom.

How does one ensure that their thoughts are right? The thoughts one has are right when they can be proven with facts and are in agreement with Life and nature. The more right thoughts we have in our minds, the less friction we experience from wrong thoughts. Right thoughts can only produce right results and vice versa. Friction is produced from opposition. Eliminating negative thoughts that oppose positive leaves room for only positive thoughts thereby creating freedom in the mind. These positive ideas will produce motion that is in harmony with nature, making one experience freedom in their motion.

This formula to producing freedom is applicable in all areas of life and on all levels of existence. Thought is the essence of all that exists, so freedom in thinking equates to freedom on all levels of existence. This reality of freedom can be achieved by consistent application of the formula and principles just outlined.

B. The Nature of Right and Wrong
Why is there such a thing as right and wrong? How can one tell with absolute certainty what is right and what is wrong?

Right and wrong exist as a result of Creation and the resulting reaction to it which produced this ongoing battle for singularity which is the reality at the root of everything we witness taking place in the universe.

Right is a pattern of thinking and motion that ensures creation remains in existence and doesn't go back to a state of nothing, with no aim, purpose or direction. This is what determines what is right or positive in life. All that works to perpetuate intelligent motion or creation is right or positive. All else is wrong or negative.

Of the two natures within us, positive and negative, whichever we promote the most by what we think and do will eventually determine the type of person we become. When we practice having and moving out on positive thoughts, all of our habits, character and circumstances will also be positive. As a man thinks so is he.

The dualities in life are manifestations of these two forces, positive and negative i.e. Right vs. wrong, Truth vs. falsehood, Order vs. chaos, Health vs. disease, Intelligence vs. foolishness, Life vs. death etc. As intelligent beings it should be our focus to do everything in our power to magnify positive or right as this promotes life and keeps us in existence. No sane person or being wants to go back into nothingness. Life is a beautiful expression of infinite possibilities and never-ending growth. For most this is not easy to realize because of a high intensity of negative on this planet at this time being expressed as the pain, suffering, chaos, wars, disease and death that we see. These negatives cloud our sight to see the beauty of life.

The people promoting wrong and perpetrating evil on their fellow men and other life are blinded by greed and a selfish want for instant, yet temporary enjoyment. This makes them lose sight of the long-term and far-reaching damage to themselves and everybody else that their actions are causing. How can an intelligent man damage the planet that he and his descendants live on for a profit? Where will he spend his wealth when the planet is gone? Why would a sane person willingly go against that which makes things go right for everybody including him? For most, it is out of greed, laziness and impatience. Greed is a result of operating under the illusion that there is a shortage of resources thereby somebody might beat them to the limited supply. So they want to get it all right now and make the most profit before anyone else. Some are lazy to put forth effort and go through all the processes that ensures everything turns out right, then exercise patience to wait for the right results to manifest. Usually unnatural methods or practices provide quicker results however with long-term detriments, while natural methods or practices seem to take longer and have long-lasting benefits.

Thinking and doing things in a manner that is in harmony with the pattern of life allows us to perform our duty to creation. Our purpose is to perform positive deeds in the world, which keeps intelligent motion going perpetually, which consequently makes Creation stay in existence.

Doing things wrong ultimately leads to death, a state of motionlessness and nothingness. Sin is the transgression of the laws of nature and this practice goes against life and leads to death. This is why it is taught that the wages of sin is death. The magnitude of one's sins is directly proportional to the rate of the process of their death. For example, the more cigarettes one smokes, the sooner and more intense their respiratory issues progress and the quicker their bodies will fail, leading to death. On the contrary, the more care one puts into ensuring they keep their thoughts positive, their motion harmonious, their bodies clean, well fed and rested, the better their bodies will perform and the longer their lives will be with little to no pain, aches and/or bruises.

The more aware we are about Life and the laws that govern thought and motion, the more willing and able we are to perform right to the best of our ability, thereby increasing the level of freedom we experience in all we do.

C. How to be Right

When one knows better they are more likely to do better. To fully equip ourselves to live life freely, we are going to explore the ways to keep our thinking right, or free of negative or wrong. There are positive thought patterns that, when adopted, will ensure we are successful in all that we do in life. Knowing an idea and applying it consistently are two different realities. This is where discipline plays a key part for us to be successful in mastering right thinking. Disciplining oneself is keeping one's word to oneself by doing what one told themselves they are going to do. For example, if one tells themselves that they are going to quit smoking by the end of the week and they control their thoughts and motion and are successful in that goal, then that is a demonstration of discipline. They gave themselves a command and successfully carried it out. They kept their word to themselves. It is going to take great discipline on our part to ensure our thoughts are consistently right. Now let us discuss some of the thought processes that will assist us in thinking right.

a) Compliance with the Laws of Nature

Our ability to think and do right or positive is determined by our level of compliance with the laws of nature. Law is a set pattern of motion that forms the foundation of the universe. These laws must be adhered to for one to experience success in any endeavor, since all thought and motion is subject to and governed by these laws. There are many laws in existence that are being demonstrated in front of us every day, like the law of gravity. Here we are going to discuss the father of all laws. The first law of nature is the law of self-preservation. Self refers to a whole which is made up of fractions or cells. Our body is an example of self, as it is made up of individual cells. A family is a form of self, composed of the various members as the cells or fractions.

To preserve is to keep in the same state or condition. As fractions of the whole, Universe, when we do things to preserve our existence, we also preserve the existence of the whole. Our very purpose is to preserve and magnify Life or Creation, which is the Self that is composed of all the fractions in the universe. In other words, everything in Creation is there for the purpose of ensuring that Life survives perpetually.

All life obeys this law, first and foremost. Animals will fight or flight to survive, trees and other plants will grow thorns and other mechanisms to survive, all of this is done in obedience to the law of self-preservation. Life is intelligent motion. Everything in creation is an expression of intelligence. Humans are the highest expression of intelligence on this planet. The first law set to keep this intelligent motion perpetual is the Law of Self Preservation. All other laws of nature are to serve this one first law. All positive attributes and expressions in Life like love, compassion, peace, order, harmony etc. are means to keep intelligent motion (Life) perpetual. The law of self-preservation satisfies the original inspiration, the purpose of life, which is perpetual intelligent motion. All laws are there to preserve this first law. Without it, everything else, all other laws have no purpose. Everything we do should be to preserve ourselves first.

Since we are part of society, it is crucial to observe the preservation of the society, because we cannot exist without society. Societies are governed by rules, morals and codes of conduct to promote harmony among members of that society. One of the first moral principles that go hand in hand with the law of self-preservation is the principle of non-aggression. No one has the moral right to inflict harm on another, therefore we should never be the aggressors. We are only justified to use violence when we are fending off an attack that is threatening our own life. When all men realize that no-one is justified to violate another or his private property, then it will be very easy to have a peaceful society. Private property is something one owns and has complete authority over, meaning he doesn't have to seek permission from somebody else to determine what he is going to do with this property as long as he is not violating the rights or sovereignty of others. Private property is something one possesses either by birthright or because they made it themselves, or got it through purchase, inheritance or donation.

If a man is not justified to use aggressive force or violence on another man or his property, neither is a group because a group derives its authority from individuals. Since no man has the moral right to rob or force anything onto his neighbor, neither is a group because no-one can delegate authority that they themselves as individuals do not have. This applies even to governments, which are groups of individuals that represent the whole. They derive their authority from individuals, and no individual can delegate authority that they themselves do not have. It is a misconception that most people have to think that certain groups in society have authority to do things that they themselves have no divine or moral right to do. Where do these groups derive this authority from to do things to people that would be considered immoral or wrong if one person was to do it to their neighbor? Any groups, including governments, only have the same authority that an individual in the society that they represent has, nothing more and nothing less, therefore they are not exempt from the non-aggression principle. Non-compliance to this non-aggression principle will indeed destroy society. Going against society is going against self, and vice versa. We should not do anything that threatens our life or the life of another.

Right thinking enables us to always be in harmony with this one law (self-preservation) by always focusing on and doing or producing only that which supports Life. The system to discern what promotes Life is the ability to think factually, so that one can tell with certainty what is right, positive, accurate, healthy, peaceful, harmonious etc. This ability will equip one to only engage in thoughts and activities that will keep them and others alive.

Sin is the transgression of the laws of nature/life, hence the statement that the wages of sin is death. When we do things that threaten our life, we are also threatening everyone's life because we are connected in many ways. When we do things that threaten the survival of society, we are also threatening our own life because we are part of society. Let us encourage each other to do only things that promote life because we were put on this planet to LIVE. We live by ensuring that all we think and do adds to life.

b) Thinking Factually

The ability to analyze and discern things as they really are, free of bias, is the first step in one being able to think and do right. Factual thinking is when all decisions and actions are based solely on information that can be verified with proof or facts. The gathering and adding up of facts in order to determine right from wrong, positive from negative, life from death, truth from falsehood etc. is the foundation of freedom. This thought process enables us to make decisions based on what can be proven to work, thereby increasing our chances of success in all we do and reducing negative incidences in our lives. The negative force thrives on illusions, or what is not, to take life off track. Most people base their decisions on personal feelings and beliefs, therefore setting themselves up for disappointment when their feelings lead them astray or their beliefs turn out to be wrong. A belief is a concept we accept as truth without proof, so it could be right or it could be wrong. This practice of operating from belief is unwise if we want to be successful in everything we do. We have to base everything we think and do on what we can prove. When we can prove something, we know it, cancelling out the need to believe.

Being able to look at only facts in any given scenario requires discipline to remain non-personal as well as control one's emotions. Being personal in a situation and having uncontrollable emotions tend to diminish clarity of thought. When people are personal, they reject or ignore facts that they find offensive to some person, especially themselves. Having insufficient facts normally results in inaccurate answers or decisions. 1+1=2 is a fact regardless to who is saying it, how they are saying it, what race, age, social class or creed they are. The ability to think factually enables us to discern with certainty what is right from wrong, or positive from negative. This awareness of what is right or positive empowers us to make choices that promote peace and harmony, guaranteeing our success in all our endeavors.

When we all start thinking factually, we will be able to view everything in life from the same base. This will enable us to agree on the best course of action in all areas of life that is in everyone's favor by promoting freedom. We all agree on 1+1=2 being a factual or mathematical statement regardless of our race, age, religion, nationality etc. Therefore looking at ideas behind everything factually gives us a common base of thought to agree on. This base ensures our success and unites us to work and live in peace and harmony.

c) Replacing Non-beneficial Programs

Utilizing our ability to think factually, we can easily look at all the programs or beliefs or concepts we use to guide our lives to see if they are producing the life that we want or not. If not, we are duty bound to replace them with new ideas that will produce the habits and results that we want in our lives. Most people have a tendency to hold on to ideas that were passed down to them by other people of influence in their lives even though they can clearly see these ideas are not serving them. We have to let go of old beliefs that are opposed to life and harmony if we intend to be free and replace them with new positive thoughts and then create activities around these new thoughts to solidify them as our new paradigm or base in our thinking. For example you might have picked up the idea of smoking cigarettes when you were young and were not thinking for yourself, and you can see now that it is harming your body and not in line with the image of health you want. Now that you are thinking for yourself and want to quit this old habit, the solution will be to find a new positive habit like exercising and then join a gym and start associating with other people who are into health and fitness to support your new habit. Before long, you will be able to drop the habit, heal your body, enhance your physical performance and start feeling better than you have ever felt in a long time.

d) Looking for What Can Be Proven

An important key idea to focus on as intelligent thought-evolved beings is to always look for the right or positive or lesson in any given situation, thing, place or person and constantly magnify that. When this is done it allows for all the right to be brought to the surface and utilized accordingly in getting an accurate assessment of what is in front of us. When we look for what makes something right and constantly explore that, if there is any wrong, it will automatically show itself. The most common tendency we have is to look for the wrong or flaw or lie in a situation, place, thing or person, unaware that by so doing we often miss the right or positive or truth or lesson. When we look for the right first, we get the positive in its entirety and any wrong will also show itself. However, when we look for the wrong first, we might miss the wrong if there is no wrong and possibly miss the right as well since that is not our focus. We have to understand this; to know what is wrong one has to know what is right. The only way to know if 1+1=3 is wrong, one has to know that 1+1=2. Right is the yardstick to determine what is wrong. This is why positive or right should be our focus. Also, one has to know the Truth in order to tell a lie. A lie hides the truth, and one cannot hide what they do not know. So looking for the right or truth or positive is the first step in any assessment of a situation, idea, motion, thing or person, because it allows us to have a clear picture of both sides, positive and negative.

e) Being Innocent

Closely tied to the idea of looking for what can be proven (right) is the idea of innocence. Innocence is the ability to always look for the right or positive in everything and everyone. One expresses innocence by being in the posture of looking for, focusing on and only accepting the truth or right in everything. This requires not having preconceived ideas about something or someone as this tends to blind us from accurately perceiving what is. We are to always explore the why of everything and then gather facts by asking questions. We should avoid the habit of making statements that express our preconceived ideas however disguised as questions. For example, when we ask somebody if they think we are over-weight, what we are actually doing is making a statement that we are over-weight and looking to see if the other person agrees with that statement or not. The proper way will be to simply ask the other person what they think about our weight, and let them express what they see without being influenced by our preconceived idea.

Our posture when we ask questions should be of one genuinely expecting to receive a truthful answer. If the answer we get doesn't add up factually then we can ask further questions while still maintaining the same posture of innocence. If someone is sharing other than truth in their response, then we let the facts show them that their answer was not truthful simply by asking further questions.

An example is of person A asking person B a question, and person B has it in their mind that person A already has the answer to that question. The right thing for person B to do will be to answer the question and then ask person A why they asked the question. If what person A shares adds up then it clears the assumption person B had otherwise if their response doesn't add up then person B should still remain innocent and ask any further questions to get clarity. It is unwise to assume why somebody is saying or doing what they are doing and then react to that assumption. What if the assumption is wrong? This habit produces disharmony in relationships of all types.

Whenever we don't understand something, it is because of a question that has come up. When the question is answered, clarity prevails. The key is keeping our minds focused on getting to the truth without being hampered by preconceived ideas that will cloud our judgment. This focus is achieved by constantly looking for what can be proven or what works. Let us practice this in our everyday interactions and see what happens.

f) Language

Language is the medium in which we formulate thoughts and ideas to communicate to ourselves and others. This medium forms a bridge between minds to exchange ideas. The best medium to communicate an idea with is the one with the most functions to cover all aspects of the idea. This ensures that the exact same picture is transferred between the minds that are communicating.

Language is a tool for communication and it serves no purpose without thoughts or ideas to communicate. Language is best used to express what is going to take place, what is needed, how it will take place, where, by whom, when and why. When language is focused on negative, it is being used to stop, hinder and cancel out the achievement of positive ideas. When language maintains the purity of the idea, the idea is most likely to get accomplished successfully by all those involved.

As individuals, our focus should be on understanding and mastering self. Language plays a critical part in this because it determines how we speak to ourselves, which determines how we receive, assimilate and move out on particular thoughts, to our benefit or detriment. Language determines our perception of reality, whether positive or negative and consequently determines our character by the habits we have based on the thoughts we let dominate our minds. Our constant "self-talk" should serve to affirm positive ideas in our minds. By constantly repeating to ourselves what we want, how we are going to achieve it and why, we build our faith in our abilities by always focusing on what we can and are going to do. When we think that we can or we cannot, we are right.

When we use positive language to speak to ourselves and others, we promote positive thoughts in our minds, thereby enabling us to act positively and create positive habits. These positive habits build our positive character with power to accomplish positive ideas with ease which results in a positive life. We are like magicians, utilizing our words to cast spells that eventually produce the results in our lives.

We should say what we mean and mean what we say. Slang or colloquial language contaminates ideas by using words that mean something different than what they are being used for. The more slang we utilize in our communications, the more confusion we generate. An example is the use of the word "kid" to refer to our children. A kid is a baby goat, and it is not wise to refer to our intelligent and beautiful children with animal terms. This practice devalues our children's importance in our eyes on a subliminal level. When we refer to everything by its proper term, we keep its value in our minds intact.

Our success in life is determined by how much we are able to get done by effectively communicating ideas to ourselves and others. Language is a key component to achieving freedom because when we use it positively, it will inspire, motivate and empower us to do, have and become anything we want in life.

g) Speaking Directly
When we share ideas with others in an indirect, round-about way, it creates room for misunderstanding and confusion to come in. In most cases, people say things indirectly hoping the other person will connect the dots and get the point they are trying to put across. This is often a result of being fearful of rejection or possible confrontation. When they share an idea indirectly, it leaves them with room to deny or change the idea if the other person responds or reacts unfavorably. This is all an illusion of course. A clear example is person A wanting a ride from person B however instead of

simply asking if he may get a ride to such and such place, he asks if person B is going in that direction. Even if person B says yes, that still doesn't answer the real question, which is if he may get a ride. This way of communicating makes the other person answer an unnecessary question and he may also start wondering why he is being asked this question. It will be better for person A to just ask if he may get a ride to whatever place he wants to go since that is what he really wants to know. This saves both of them time and energy by making the dialogue short and direct. Speaking directly ensures our interactions are harmonious and purposeful.

As an exercise, let us analyze our own interactions with others and discipline ourselves to say exactly what we want to relay to others and ask directly what we want to know. Let us also assist others to do the same when they come to us and speak to us indirectly about anything and explain to them how much freedom they will experience when they adopt this practice of speaking directly.

h) The Three Keys to Success
The three fundamental keys to success and freedom in any endeavor are to always check, never assume and be specific. When one checks, they are verifying that what they are moving out on or basing their decisions on is factual. It is a well-known fact that most major man-made disasters in life are results of somebody somewhere somehow moving out on assumptions. This is evident in our own life experiences. Assuming is taking a thought or idea we have as a fact without verifying it with proof (facts). When this happens and the thought or idea is wrong then we have to face uncomfortable results of our assumptions. An example is assuming that a car we are driving has enough fuel and engine oil, so we do not bother to check these things to make sure we have enough. When we find ourselves

stranded on the highway because we ran out of fuel or the engine failed due to lack of oil, then we only have ourselves to blame for not checking. When we always check, we never have to assume.

Being specific is also crucial, especially dealing with other people. When we relay non-specific information or instructions to someone, the chances of them carrying out the instruction successfully are greatly diminished. For example, if we send someone to buy a pair of shoes however we do not specify the size, color or style we want, most likely what they bring back will not be what we had in mind or want. It is the consistency in doing ordinary things like always checking, never assuming and being specific that will make ordinary people like you and me extra ordinary. Again, let us adopt this practice immediately and witness the level of freedom in our everyday motion increase dramatically.

i) Magnification
Another simple habit to develop and practice to ensure our thinking and motion is right is to magnify that motion in our minds and see if it still promotes peace and life. In essence, whatever we are planning to do, imagine more and more people doing the same thing. If it still produces harmony with others then it is right. When it starts producing friction as more people outside of us adopt the same thinking and motion, then it is most probably not the right thing for us to do. Take for example you are in a home with others and about to eat together. There is a pot of soup and it is clear everyone is going to want some of this soup and you are the first one to take your portion. To ensure that everyone gets a fair share and there is no conflict, you could use the process of magnification to see if everyone was to get the same portion as you, will there be enough soup for everyone or

not. If not, then you will need to make adjustments to your portion to make sure there is enough soup left for everyone to get the same portion as you, which is the right thing to do.

D. Stumbling Blocks to Avoid

In the following sections, we are going to address a few stumbling blocks in our thinking that cause freedom to elude us. These ideas are reactions to truth or right, and prevent us from accepting the truth or right in the form of correction, so that we can apply it in our quest to be free from wrong. These ideas manifest in our minds in various forms when correction or elevation is being given so that we can change and grow. Explanations, examples and exercises will be shared to assist us in this transition to a new thinking that produces freedom.

a) Being Defensive

The first stumbling block is being defensive. Defense is when a correction is given and one starts thinking of ways to defend or justify the wrong in what they said or did. Regardless of how one might think they were justified, the idea or motion is still wrong and the defense does not make it right. This thought process of defending wrong is a result of the negative force utilizing our ego, the "I", to hide itself so that it is not exposed for what it is thereby avoiding being removed or replaced in the individual's mind with positive. This is the ego trying to avoid shame and guilt. When one is thinking right and looking to grow in their ability to think accurately and do right, they are open to correction. So when they are in error and someone brings it to their attention, their focus is on the right/truth that they are to apply to be right and exact in the future. When this is done, shame and guilt do not come up. Whatever it is one does in error or by mistake, they are to look at the lesson, explore the why and what needs to be known and done to make sure everything goes right next time. When one gets the lesson they get the blessing of elevation.

Here is a scenario we are going to use to illustrate the stumbling blocks being discussed here. Say there are two people, John and James, sharing an apartment and utilizing the same fridge to store their food. One afternoon John comes home thirsty however he doesn't have any more bottled water so he drinks James' last bottle. James returns home in the evening thirsty and when he goes to retrieve his last bottle, it is gone. He asks John if he drank his water to which John admits. James explains how that was not the right thing to do and John says he was thirsty and since he had no more water he just drank what was in the fridge. John goes on to say since James has helped himself to some of his food and drinks before, he thought it was fine for him to help himself to James' water. The posture John has is that of defending his actions, even though it is clear he is wrong and his actions are producing friction between the two. We are going to discuss the correct posture John should have in later sections.

b) Being Personal
Being personal is the second stumbling block, and this is when one focuses at a person instead of the idea being discussed. When one is in error and correction is brought to them and instead of acknowledging and accepting the correction (truth/right) they focus on the person bringing the correction or any other person involved in the scenario which does not change the idea of the correction then that is an expression of being personal. This habit is also expressed when one defends another's wrong because they like the person and feel if they accept the fact that the person is in error or made a mistake, that might mess up their relationship. So, due to fear, they try to protect the person

46

they are fond of by defending their wrong in the face of facts showing otherwise. Usually the defense comes by trying to shift the attention from the wrong by focusing on other things that might be positive and factual yet do not negate the error or mistake. This also does not cancel out the need for a change in the person's thinking to make sure they do not repeat the same transgression in the future.

Utilizing the same scenario with James and John, their neighbor comes over to watch a game as they normally do and witnesses the dialogue. The neighbor inserts himself and explains to John that regardless to past events, the right thing to do will have been to check with James if he could have his last water bottle this way it would not have been a surprise to James. In response, John shares with the neighbor that he has no business in their conversation since he doesn't live there. This is an example of John being personal, focusing the attention on the person of the neighbor instead of the validity of the idea being expressed. It is about the validity of an idea, and not who is sharing it.

c) Being Technical
The third idea that blocks many from perceiving and accepting truth or right is being technical. This is when one focuses and magnifies a certain part of an idea as if that part is the most important and therefore changes the entire idea. This is also an attempt to change or take away attention from the truth, which will make one feel justified in not accepting the entire idea in a correction.

In the same scenario above, the neighbor shares with John that it is not right for him to steal and then guzzle someone's water without checking. John responds by saying that is not correct because he did not steal the water nor did he guzzle it. That statement doesn't change the fact that the idea in what the neighbor is sharing is accurate that John should have checked before taking anything that doesn't belong to him. John is trying to invalidate what the neighbor said by magnifying parts of what he said as if those parts will change the whole idea. That is an example of being technical. It would be proper for John to explore the right in the idea and submit to it, and if he would like his neighbor to refine his language he may share it after recognizing and submitting to the truth in the correction.

Being defensive, personal, and technical are the main reasons why most interactions between people end up in chaos and confusion. When everyone thinks factually, it enables all to arrive at decisions and conclusions in unison. However when others do not want to accept certain facts, it is mainly because of the three ideas mentioned above. Either they do not like the person bearing the truth or the way the person is presenting the truth or they do not want to be seen as being wrong. Wise people accept truth even when it is coming from a dog.

These erroneous thought patterns can be avoided when we keep certain positive ideas at the forefront of our minds to enhance our ability to see and accept truth or right. The first idea is to always look for what is right or true or factual or positive in what is being expressed or done. This way we are more apt to see the idea or purpose behind a thing first, and then any wrong will automatically show itself. We don't have to go look for wrong. When we look for wrong, we miss the right or truth. The second idea to focus on is being solution-oriented by exploring to see what we can do now or in the future or could have done to make things go right. This ensures we are always open to learn and grow by improving ourselves. Last point to keep in mind when receiving correction from another is to question any thought that comes to our mind. Will the thought change or add to what is being expressed? If not then it is not necessary to explore or share it. What will be the point?

E. Accepting Correction

To easily accept correction without letting being defensive, personal and technical get in the way, imagine you dropped a $100 bill and the person bringing the correction to you is the one who noticed you dropped the money and is bringing it to your attention. Regardless to who they are, what or how they say it, will that be your focus or will you just be thankful that they found your money and happy to get it back? For most of us we will just be happy to get the money and will not be bothered by who the person is or what they said or how they said it. Corrections make us better people, and that is more valuable than any amount of money, so we should always be eager to accept being corrected and be thankful that somebody cared enough to share a correction with us regardless to what we think their motive might be.

Here is another way to view and accept correction properly. Imagine you are driving somewhere and then you run into someone who brings to your attention that you are going in the wrong direction. Will it be wise for you to continue going in the same wrong direction because you have already drove 500 miles in that direction, or because you do not like that person or what they said and how they said it? Should you even be questioning their motive if you can see that the person is pointing you in the right direction? In real life we would say one is insane in this situation if they refuse the correction, yet most people do this almost every day when simple corrections are brought to their attention. Instead of simply accepting a correction that will help us grow, we spend a lot of time and energy focusing on who brought the correction, what they said, how they said it, what could be the motive behind it etc. Our focus should be on seeing how the correction applies, and if it does, we should adopt and apply it from that point forward because it will add to our level of freedom. Even more importantly, we should be grateful for the correction and the person who brought it to us regardless as to who they are, what they said, how they said it, or the motive behind them sharing it. What we know is that the correction has added to our growth and that is a positive thing. Even if they shared the correction to spite us, we should not waste our time and energy pursuing that as long as the correction is valid and has benefitted us. This practice makes other people comfortable sharing corrections or recommendations for improvement with us, which only accelerates our growth into freedom.

F. Self-Awareness

Are you aware of who or what you are? What method does one employ to determine who or what they are?

Most of us identify ourselves with ideas, thought patterns and habits we picked up from those we associate with and start to think that is who we are by nature, to the point of defending it. This is understandable however grossly flawed. We get to see our real selves when we think right and live by and practice Truth or Right. This means doing things based on intelligence and with proper understanding of what we are doing and why. When we think positively and do what we feel inspired to do that benefit the whole, then we start seeing our real character – the way we carry the truth. When we pick up habits from others involuntarily, like celebrities, we are not being ourselves and people will not see our true unique character until we start doing what is right for the right reason.

Defending habits and expressions we adopted from others that we don't even understand stops us from changing and growing into who we really are. When we do this we are merely living an illusion. We have to remember that imitation is indeed suicide. Those copied habits are not us by design or nature, therefore have to be discarded in order for us to discover and reveal our true selves to ourselves and the world.

Couples, friends etc. who do not inspire each other to grow into better yet authentic versions of themselves, are cheating themselves of the true benefits of relationships. We are meant to be each other's mirrors in our growth and development.

We are designed to grow constantly. Anything that doesn't grow is dead. Life is all about growth, elevation, and change. Our understanding is always deepening. We should strive to grow and change into better and more aware beings. When we know better we are more apt to do better. So as our awareness expands our habits and characters change to reflect that growth. We should always look forward to changing and growing. When we stop growing we start dying.

Do you realize that there is a thought behind everything everybody says or does? To see the Truth of all that you say and do, ask the question WHY and explore it until there is no more WHY questions to ask, then you have gotten to the thought, the essence of YOU. This way you can change what is not right by replacing it with that which is positive or right, and the more you do it the more the creative force in you starts coming out. When we do this we become conscious creators and will be able to erect a civilization that our descendants will be proud of. It is in our power to do.

So, let us strive to always be aware of our thoughts and the motive behind everything we do. This way we will be more aware of ourselves and have better control of our lives.

G. Common Flawed Thought Patterns

We have numerous common and widely practiced thought patterns that are flawed and keep us in the bondage of ignorance. These thought patterns are defense mechanisms our ego mounts against correction or elevation from wrong thinking to right thinking. They make us feel justified to hold on to ideas that are against right. A clear example is with someone who smokes and they know smoking is an unnatural habit that is slowly but surely killing their body, which makes it wrong, however they keep doing it. What are they telling themselves to justify this habit? In essence one has to lie to themselves to feel comfortable doing something they know is wrong.

These are some of the common thought patterns:

- I am my own person

- There is no absolute right or wrong, what is wrong to someone is not wrong to another

- What I do is my own business

- Let us agree to disagree

- You do you and I do me

- I am free to express myself

- Everyone is entitled to their own opinion

- I do what feels right or good to me

These few examples are thoughts that are aimed at nullifying truth. Truth is absolute and can easily be defined. It is also very simple to see, yet we have many who make it seem very complicated. Complication comes from trying to make truth fit with the lies, or when we try to use right to justify wrong. The worst liar is one who lies to himself. When one is courageous enough to tell themselves the truth, most likely they may change and start being right. However when they lie to themselves saying that what they are doing is right when they know it is wrong, then the chances of them putting forth energy to change their wrong thinking are greatly reduced. When one lies to themselves, even if they tell others the truth, they will most likely not change and that wrong they do not change will bring them hardships later and eventually bring about their demise. The rate of their dying process will be equivalent to the magnitude of their wrong. For example, the more you smoke cigarettes, the quicker the consequences will catch up with you and the more intense the discomfort will be.

Here are some ideas to address these common flawed thought patterns:

1. When one says I am my own person, they are attempting to alienate themselves from everybody and make themselves believe that the same laws of nature that govern everyone else do not apply to them, even though facts show this is not true. We are all subjects to the same laws and no one is exempt from abiding by these laws, nor is there the slightest tolerance for ignorance of these laws.

2. What we think determines what we do and what we do will eventually affect everyone else outside of us. When we think positively our positive actions will affect others positively and vice versa. For example when one smokes, they are supporting a business that is against life and health and the

smoke affects others negatively as second hand smoking. Also the odor we give off offends most non-smokers. As our health begins to suffer, everything and everyone around us is affected by our lack of physical performance, then add to that the stress from watching us in pain. So the notion that what we think and do is our own business is an illusion, an untruth. Our thoughts are everyone's business as they will affect everyone, positively or negatively. We are affected today by noble thoughts of past and present visionaries, inventors, artists etc. just as we are also affected by wicked thoughts of past and present criminals like tyrants, slave masters, murderers, robbers etc.

3. Agreeing to disagree is a common thought that is expressed when one party is unwilling to accept truth from the other party. When both parties utilize factual thinking, then it should be easy to arrive at the same conclusion in unison just as we all agree that 1+1=2. Whenever there is a disagreement it shows either parties are operating from a wrong thought or one party is right and the other is wrong. It is never the case that both parties are right however just cannot see eye to eye. Truth is one.

4. Opinions are thoughts we have that are not verified with facts. They are either right or wrong. When a thought can be proven, then it is a fact. When we practice factual or right thinking, we put opinions to the side and deal with facts to arrive at definite conclusions and or make right decisions. Most people have made themselves to believe that there is nothing absolute, not even facts. So they think their opinions are just as valid as facts. When someone expresses truth or facts they lie to themselves that it is merely someone's opinion which means they don't have to accept it. Stating that smoking is unhealthy and will cause respiratory issues in the body is a fact and not an opinion. Just because

somebody takes it as an opinion doesn't negate it being a fact. People can express their opinions however opinions become invalid in the face of FACTS (that which can be proven).

5. We are to do right because it is right to do. What makes it right to do is because of the positive benefits that are rendered to all things. For example when we all refrain from smoking, we have more funds to spend on meaningful things. Also, our health is better, the air is cleaner for everyone, and we have more time and energy to do things that benefit us and others. Even though smoking may make us feel pleasurable sensations temporarily, it will make us and those close to us suffer later, so it is an unhealthy practice.

H. Being Thorough

Understanding an idea or system completely equips us with power to ensure the idea or system runs smoothly and successfully. This entails familiarizing ourselves with other ideas or systems that are connected to the idea or system. When we know everything about a system and how it affects and is affected by other systems connected to it, then we understand it thoroughly.

When correcting something, we are to also check all systems connected to the failed system to ensure any flaws that could have contributed to the failure or other systems that could have been affected as well are corrected. We are to look at everything as ONE.

For example if one is fixing a broken fuel line on a car, one has to investigate why the line broke in the first place. By examining systems connected to the fuel line, one can see what triggered this mishap and also if anything else was affected. This is the same with analyzing events and conditions before a certain occurrence as well as possible future outcomes that will be a result of this occurrence. When we view our individual selves as a system connected to other systems, we start viewing reality in a more complete and thorough manner. This empowers us to live in harmony with all. When we are in harmony with all, we are free to accomplish our ideas successfully by having the support of everything and everyone.

I. Positive Habits to Develop

To produce and perpetuate peace and freedom, certain habits have to be developed through practice. To make a practice a habit, one has to understand the idea behind the practice and have the will to internalize that idea through consistent application of the idea. Perfect practice makes perfect, for example learning to master playing a musical instrument. One has to dedicate time and energy to serious practice if they intend to become proficient at playing that particular instrument. The more one practices the idea, the more that idea becomes a habit and eventually becomes part of their character. Character is how one carries the Truth. Since the application of truth determines the level of freedom one experiences, one has to be versatile in the way they carry and apply truth. This equates to one having a strong character that affects life positively and is capable of accomplishing many ideas almost effortlessly. The more positive habits one has, the more versatile they are to move in and out of any situation without causing or experiencing friction, which equates to more freedom. Our experiences in life teach us lessons that make us grow in character. At the base of everything we go through in life is an opportunity to apply, understand and master one or more of these positive attributes like love, patience, loyalty, happiness, compassion, gentleness, trust, honesty, humility, openness etc.

The base of all these positive attributes is righteousness, meaning right or truth in motion. These attributes work to produce and maintain harmony and freedom in life. We are going to discuss some of these positive attributes here.

Love is lowering oneself to serve another when you don't have to. When one loves another, they think and do things that bring pleasure and comfort to the one they love. The greatest way to express love to someone is by sharing with them the truth. Truth gives one who values it understanding, which equates to peace of mind as well as an increased awareness of how to live life more harmoniously. The more truth one knows, the more ideas one is able to accomplish successfully in life without friction, therefore being free. Let us also keep in mind that when you love someone, you want the best for them. You want them to be comfortable, cared for, experience pleasure and be respected. You value them, their thoughts, and believe in their dreams, even when you do not understand them. Now, can you give something you don't have? Charity begins at home. So for you to say you love someone, you have to understand that concept, and the best person to practice that attribute on constantly is self. Self-love is the beginning of proper appreciation of Life and everything and everybody in it. When we understand that we attract to ourselves that which we are, then how can we properly love what we have attracted, other people, when we lack love for what attracted it, ourselves? It is one in the same. In essence, we have to love ourselves first and foremost so that we may know and understand how to love everybody else. The things you would NOT let those you love eat, dress in, or have around them, should not exist around YOU either. So feed, clothe, shelter and treat yourself the way you would those you love and see what happens.

Trust is the ability to depend on the accuracy of another's thinking and motion to the point of allowing them to think or carry out certain ideas for you. The more one shows a track record of thinking and doing things accurately, the more that one can be trusted. We want to consistently practice thinking and doing right so that we become worthy of being trusted by others.

Loyalty is the ability to dedicate oneself to the accomplishment of an idea. The greatest idea to express loyalty towards is Truth or Life, and when one is loyal to life, they make sure all their thoughts and motion is in harmony with everything in Creation. This gives them increased freedom to interact with life successfully. When one is loyal to other people's ideas which are right, they make it possible for others to become loyal to them and their ideas as well. People who are not loyal usually will not be trusted, which will limit the level of participation or details of a particular idea or motion they are privileged to, thereby limiting their freedom in said idea or motion. The more loyal one is, the more they develop a track record that will allow them to be trusted. The more one is trusted the more details they will be allowed to know pertaining to the idea or motion they are participating in. This greatly increases their level of freedom in said idea or motion and in life in general.

Honesty is expressed when one is open and truthful in their thoughts and deeds. An honest person truthfully expresses their thoughts and the motives behind their deeds are open. Honesty creates trust, respect and harmony between parties in relationships. These are ingredients for one to experience freedom since they remove potential friction in interactions with others. Friction in relationships usually arises from absence of trust, respect and harmony due to lack of honesty.

Humility is when one postures themselves to receive and be elevated, which is the right posture for learning new ideas. The more ideas one learns the more power one has at their disposal to apply to achieve success in any given endeavor. As previously stated, when we know better, we are more likely to do better. Proper application of our knowledge gives us more freedom in what we do. The more we know about a particular thing, the more we know what to do in order to interact harmoniously with said thing.

Anyone who humbles themselves to be taught, and then apply what they were taught to the point of mastery will gain much freedom in that idea by knowing how to think and act in order to be successful in accomplishing that idea with little to no difficulty.

Gratitude is an emotion generated from the thought of being thankful. Gratitude allows us to see the value in something or someone and be appreciative of having that thing or person in our experience. This expression of gratitude puts us in sync with the Source of all things and opens up channels for more to be given to us. When we are in the vibration or feeling of gratitude, we automatically free ourselves from the grip of any negative emotion or feeling. Gratitude is known as the aristocrat of positive emotions. It puts us in a high vibration, which automatically dissipates negative feelings the same way darkness immediately disappears when light shows up. We should develop gratitude as an everyday attitude by repeating to ourselves the things we are grateful for throughout the day and watch our days turn brighter and brighter as we discover more things to be grateful for.

Patience is the motion of paying now for what we will receive later. The quality of our patience is determined by the level of our knowledge. The more knowledge we have, the greater our ability to express patience. When we give time, energy, and resources to an idea, that idea will return to us what we put in it. The longer we wait before collecting what is ours, the more time the idea has to magnify what we have given in the course of its development. The more time we allow for the magnification of the idea, the greater our rewards. By exercising patience, we free ourselves from unnecessary negative expressions like stress, anxiety and frustration as we await our goals in life to manifest.

J. Further Expansion of Awareness

Mathematically speaking, the degree of freedom we will experience in our life is the measure of the level of our awareness. The more we are aware of, the more we are able to do or be without restraint. The more we are able to do and be, the more life we can express and experience. The more life we are expressing, the more freedom we are demonstrating. So, in essence, freedom is the ability to express life, and is determined by our level of awareness. In the following sections we are going to expand our awareness by factually exploring certain aspects of life that need to be understood better for us to experience life more freely.

a) Know Thyself
Who and What We Are

Everything is energy and all is a manifestation of thought. Thought is energy directed. We are what we think therefore we are thought, making us energy at our essence. Our souls or entities are masses of ideas. Our purpose is to magnify life or creation through expressing the ideas that are us. Life or Creation is intelligent motion. The Creator is the totality of all positive ideas and we are fractions of this Creator. We fulfill our purpose by doing what makes us happy that is in agreement with nature and promotes life and peace. Our purpose is to add to the pleasure, comfort and happiness of the world by serving those around us. After finding what makes us happy that adds to life, we are to develop a vision for our life that is in line with our purpose, and then set goals to realize this vision. Our vision is what we look to accomplish in our lifetime. We should then start seeing ourselves already doing, having and being what we want and go into motion accomplishing these goals one task at a time in a way that promotes life and peace.

The more aware we are about what makes things work right in creation, the laws of the universe, the more freedom we will experience fulfilling our life's purpose when we harmonize our thoughts and motion with these laws. Everything we do and have in life is for what we become. Our experiences with the people, situations and things in our journey of life are to expand our awareness along the way. We should look for what our motion is developing in us rather than focus on the end result. So, what we become is what is more important than what we did or how many things we accumulated in the course of our life. It is what we become that we take with us everywhere, even upon passing, everything else we leave behind.

Another way to understand what we are is viewing the human as a computer and our thoughts as software programs. Our bodies are biological computer instruments that are driven and controlled by our minds which are a collection of thoughts or programs. Our level of awareness equals the number of instructions in our software programs. The more aware we are about our bodies, the more instructions in our software programs to run and control the computer. When our awareness grows beyond the functions of our current bodies, then the body has to evolve to enable us to express all the possibilities we are capable of.

We are self-programming programs by design. We program our subconscious minds through self-talk and the ideas or pictures we pay attention to, real or imagined. The subconscious mind in turn projects these thoughts or programs (images or vibrations) into our objective reality as in a virtual reality setup. Our physical reality is a simulation of the programs running in our subconscious mind. We are in full control of our reality and circumstances. What we focus on the most is programmed into our subconscious mind and then projected into our physical reality. We have to utilize our programming skills wisely to create a reality we will actually enjoy experiencing and that will help us and others in our reality to grow into more aware beings of light. All of life is about perpetual growth and expansion of our awareness while we do what brings us the most joy and also adds to the joy of others far and near.

Will

Will is the force behind thought, or our ability to focus our attention and energy on a given thought in order to manifest it. Will is a product of a want. The greater our want for something, the more willing we are to accomplish or attain it. The more willing we are the easier it is to focus on said goal and the more opportunities we will see on how to achieve it. Whatever we really want, we are willing to do what it takes to get it, and where there is a will there is a way. Question is: What do you really want? The more willing we are to accomplish a goal, the clearer the way to its attainment.

Proper use of the will is practicing focusing our attention on positive things that are in alignment with what we want to achieve in Life. When we use our power of focus to keep our thoughts and actions in the direction of the development of our goals, instead of wanting to control other people or things outside of us, then we will experience much success in what we do.

Regarding free will, the keyword in "free will" is FREE. Free Will is the will that lead us to experience FREEDOM. Freedom is a reality void of friction or negative. One can only express free will when they are being right or positive, meaning operating in harmony with Nature. When we choose positive ideas and activities that we love or that make us happy to focus our attention on, then we are exercising free will properly. Humanity as a whole is not expressing free will. Most have lost it by giving in to wrong or negative and now their own will power is being used against them. In other words, the negative force in us makes us focus our attention on things that are opposed to our own existence and the achievement of our highest dreams.

Education

There is a saying that the only thing that is a man is his mind and everything else can be found in a pig or a horse. Since we are our minds, the most valuable education any intelligent being (ME and YOU) can have is knowledge of all the functions of their minds and how to employ them at will to produce any reality they want. We have 6 mental faculties; Perception (our point of view), Intellect/Reason (our ability to gather and add up facts to draw conclusions), Will (our ability to focus on one idea), Intuition (our internal guidance system linking us to universal intelligence), Imagination (our ability to hold images in our minds), and Memory (our ability to store & retrieve information). How many of these can you use at will? Can you imagine what you would be able to do if all these faculties where fully active? These mental muscles require exercising to stay in shape. The more one exercises them, the stronger they get and the greater the results in one's life.

Here are some simple exercises for your mind. For perception, which is how you view reality, exercise looking at only the positive or right or benefit or good in everything. Whatever you focus on you attract, so use your perception to focus on positive so that later you can only attract the good that you deserve. For the intellect, form a habit of doing puzzles which will strengthen your reasoning abilities to enable you to assess situations and ideas more accurately. To strengthen the will, practice meditations where you hold a single picture in your mind and only focus on that picture without having your mind wandering. The more you practice, the better you will become. Intuition can be exercised by learning to relax your body, and quieting your mind by taking a few breaths, and then asking yourself questions and paying attention to your body as well as the thoughts and images that come to mind. Everyone has different experiences, so you have to pay attention to yourself and see which expression your higher self utilizes to communicate with your conscious mind. It could be through a voice, visually, bodily sensations for yes or no answers or a combination of these. To develop our imagination, we have to practice seeing ourselves doing, having and being what we want as if we have already achieved it. The imagination allows us to experience things in our minds before we actually have them physically. For memory, we have to practice making unique associations of the information we want to remember with ideas or symbols we are well familiar with, like associating the names of new people we meet with our family members or car models. There are quite a few books out there to help you with developing your mental faculties and they are worth the investment. The more you exercise, the more proficient you become at expressing these faculties and the better your life will be.

Faith

Faith can be defined as the expectation of a possibility based on a proven track record. One can have faith in something happening or in the ability of somebody accomplishing a given idea based on facts from a previous occurrence or their past accomplishments. The strength of one's faith is dependent upon the amount of facts that support the track record. Our faith in something unseen is a direct result of the evidence in the seen that points to that unseen. It is easy to have faith in the rain season starting in April if the rain season has always begun in April for the past 20 or so years, just as it would be easy to have faith in a friend keeping their word to pick you up to go to work if they have always picked you up punctually for the past few years without fail. Having faith in a person or phenomena that you have no proven track record on is unwise. This is blind faith. Faith and trust go hand in hand.

The foremost person to have faith in is oneself. We have had too many successes in our lives not to have faith in ourselves accomplishing anything we want. We mastered talking, walking, running and a host of other feats that we now take for granted. Just by you being able to read and understand the ideas in this book means you have mastered the art and science of reading and comprehension to a high degree. The same process that enabled you to gain this level of mastery is applicable in gaining mastery in all other areas of life that you might decide to venture into in order to achieve your dreams.

When we develop faith in our abilities to do, have and become anything we want, then we will let go of fear, doubt and disbelief in ourselves. These three constructs undermine our limitless power within. Fear is a negative emotion we experience that paralyzes us from making forward motion because of operating in the unknown. Because we do not know our own power, we are fearful to go and try out new things we haven't tried before. Doubt is a negative emotion we experience due to lack of ability to gather and add up facts to support a given idea, so we question its validity or doubt it. When we forget our past successes and what we have already mastered and only focus on present challenges, we start doubting our ability to achieve what we want. Disbelief is another emotion we experience when we reject facts or truth in order to stay in our comfort zone. We resort to disbelieving or rejecting the truth about our inherent power because we feel by accepting that truth, it puts an obligation on us to move out of our comfort zone. What we fail to understand in that moment is that our current comfort zone used to be an unknown territory before. If we had not ventured out we would not know what we now know nor would we be experiencing the growth of awareness we now have. Everything seems difficult at first, and most things appear impossible until we actually do them.

Fear, doubt and disbelief are negative pulls on us as a result of lack of faith in our natural abilities to achieve anything we can imagine. Think of it this way, we are currently displaying great power by unknowingly manifesting the life we are currently experiencing. What more can we manifest when we have unwavering faith in our ability to do, have and be anything we want? Like scriptures teach, with faith the size of a mustard seed, we can move mountains.

What We See We Attract

It has been said that what we see and dislike the most in others are usually the same issues we are struggling with ourselves. This reality is a result of us recognizing something in others that we are aware of by having dealt with it in ourselves before. Because we are aware of it, it is easy to recognize, and because we have confronted it before, we already have an energy built up against it from prior internal struggles with the issue. We then direct this energy at others when we find or think we see the same trait/habit in them. Wise people look to correct in themselves what they see and dislike in others.

We see what we describe. How we view the world defines who we are, our thoughts. Our description of the world around us is a description of the world within us. What we see outside is a mirror of what is inside us. When one sees joy, love, peace, happiness, opportunities, abundance etc. in the world outside, they are seeing what is already in them. What we look at is what it is, however we give it meaning based on our own thoughts, our own understanding of reality. Positive people see positive all around them and vice versa. The vibration of what we see in our thoughts dictates our feelings, which dictate our actions and which in turn produces our results. In other words, we are to be the change that we want to see in the world by changing the thoughts or images in our minds.

Control and Choices

The only control we have is control over our own thoughts and behavior. We can influence others by what we say or do however we cannot control them. It is also important to know that nobody outside of us has the power to influence our thoughts unless we permit it. When we get irritated by others, it is a form of weakness on our part by allowing someone's behavior to disrupt our inner peace. When somebody does something we see can be done better, we can choose to teach or remind them of the right way to do it or not. If they do not take heed of the correction or recommendation we can choose to remove ourselves from their company so that their incongruent behavior does not affect us negatively. When we choose to look at the flaws of others as opportunities for growth it empowers us to exercise patience and compassion and free us from irritation.

Blaming others for our misfortunes is due to a lack of understanding that we are where we are in life as a direct result of the choices we have made. If one decides to hang out with people who find pleasure in disrespecting and mistreating others, they should not blame anyone when they find themselves involved in unnecessary altercations or similar uncomfortable situations. Another man can only do to us what we permit him based on our choices. We have the power to make choices that are always in our favor by thinking positively. The laws of nature serve everybody and when we know how to use them to our advantage, our destiny or fate will always be determined by us and not by someone outside of us.

Each time we have a decision or choice to make, we have an opportunity to properly apply everything we have learned in our lifetime. We are always making choices, and we always have a choice. Even when we think we are choosing not to choose, that is still a choice. Our life as it is right now is the sum total of all the choices we have made, and our choices are our responsibility and nobody else's. Other people might influence our choices, however they cannot control them.

Our level of awareness dictates the types of choices we make in every area of our life, which consequently determines the circumstances in our life. When we constantly make choices based on facts and intelligence, it will reflect in more harmonious circumstances and conditions in our reality. We should always look at everything in our life as it is and look to understand our choices that brought us to the present moment, and find the lesson in it for our growth.

Fear

Most of us are living in fear. Fear means far and faded away. When our thoughts are further away from the truth we experience fear and the more into the unknown we are, the greater the fear. This is a paralyzing feeling because in this state we are unaware of what to do, so we freeze. Fear is a product of our imagination. We imagine bad things happening in the future so we become afraid of the future. We imagine we are going to fall so we are fearful of heights. We imagine the plane is going to crash so we are fearful of flying. The more we examine the things we think we are afraid of, the more we will realize it is all imagined and we are reacting to these imaginations. The solution in this case is to use our imagination to create the scenarios that we want. When we imagine everything going right instead of going wrong, then there is nothing to be fearful of. Our fear turns into great anticipation and excitement. The more we know about a thing, situation or person, the more comfortable we are when interacting with it or them. For example people who are highly knowledgeable about snakes or lions are not fearful interacting with them at close range while most people who are not knowledgeable are fearful of these creatures. The more we don't know the more fearful we are. Knowledge removes fear.

Time

Time is one subject that is least understood by many and has a tremendous effect on how people view life, for better or for worse. Time is a formula to measure the motion it takes to complete an idea. When we say one year, we are measuring the motion of the planet rotating completely around the sun. When we say one day we are measuring the motion it takes for the planet to rotate completely on its axis. The same principle applies with clocks, they are devices with components in motion that we use to determine the length of a second, minute, or an hour. Then we apply these measurements to other motions like driving somewhere, growing and developing from birth to death etc.

This calculation of time has most people thinking that we are coming from somewhere, the past, and going somewhere, the future. In reality there is always now, and the past and the future are merely constructs in our minds in relationship to our current motion here and now. The past is not a place we came from, we have always been here and the past is a collection of events and experiences that took place here and now and only exist in our memory. The future is also a place in our minds that holds ideas we look to accomplish, and we will only accomplish those ideas here and now after we are completed with the current motion we are involved in we call today, or present moment. When we understand that all we have is now, we will learn to value and pay close attention to everything that is taking place right now because it is what actually matters and gives any meaning to everything else in the past and in the future. We only experienced the past when it was the present moment and now it is dead, and we will only experience the future when it becomes the present moment.

Our minds, for the most part, are focused on the past or the future while the present moment is going unnoticed and this produces a lot of negative experiences for us by not paying attention and properly executing what we are doing in the present moment. Most of us experience regret, shame and guilt when we think of the past because of things we did or did not do due to our lack of focus in the present moment when that past motion was here and now. Focusing on the future produces anxiety and stress for those who are not fully utilizing the resources in the present moment to prepare for that future motion so that they can execute it properly when it comes into the present moment. We should free ourselves from all these negatives by focusing on the present moment so that we can properly apply the lessons from our past in what we are doing which will raise our awareness so that we can plan for new experiences and be adequately prepared to enjoy them when the future motion with those experiences is here and now.

Since time is a measurement of the motion it takes to manifest an idea, the more aware we are about what makes things go right, the less time it will take us to do, have and become anything we want. In that sense, time is inversely proportional to the degree of freedom in any given motion. In other words, the less time it takes us to accomplish an idea, the more freedom is being expressed in that motion. So in essence, the less negative we encounter in any motion, the less time and the higher the degree of freedom we experience. This is also illustrated in the popular saying that time flies when we are having fun. When people are at a function having a wonderful time, 5 hours will seem like 30 minutes, while on the other hand somebody in excruciating pain for 10 minutes will think they have been in pain for 10 hours. So when it comes to our lives, we have to apply this awareness of time to our advantage starting now.

We are to create the picture of our ideal life and know that this reality in our minds will be our present moment experience soon. Then we set out to manifest it by intelligently applying all the lessons from our past experiences to do everything right in the present moment. Knowing that we are still the same exceptional individuals who mastered walking, talking, running etc. and that power and ability to accomplish anything we will is still with us right here right now. This should fortify our faith in our ability to bring that reality of our ideal life into the present moment. When we fully involve ourselves in everything we are doing right now to bring about our ideal future, we will enjoy every moment of it. The time that we might have thought is too long before we achieve our goals will cease to exist. When our goals are realized and we are finally enjoying the life of our dreams, time will literally be non-existent as we start experiencing a life where we have very little negative experiences and every day is an excitingly great adventure.

b) Culture

Culture is a system of living designed to cultivate, develop and promote a particular thinking and behavior in people who are part of it. The root word in culture is cult, which is a distinct group of people who practice a certain lifestyle. Everyone on the planet operates from a certain thinking and behavior and has others who identify with the same mindset and behavior. So, it must be understood that everyone has a culture and therefore belongs to some type of cult. Cultures come in many shapes and forms just as there are different ideas and activities in the world. We have the pop culture from people who relate to each other based on the thoughts and ways promoted through pop music. We have religion, politics, sports etc. and their respective cultures. Since people are involved in various activities in life, they are part and therefore expressions of a medley of cultures, therefore forming cultures within cultures. For example, one can be a college student who is European, Christian, democratic, loves hip-hop music, is ecologically-aware, and into computer-hacking, among other things. Almost every activity in their life has a distinct culture and now all these cultures are blended together in one individual.

Because every culture is rooted in its own beliefs and practices, the ideas behind it are worth exploring to ensure they produce and promote freedom for the individuals who practice them as well as everybody else. All ideas either produce and promote or oppose freedom.

Examples of ideas that have a great likelihood to hinder the attainment of freedom are religion and politics. This is because of their tendency to divide people and turn them against each other which produces tension and friction in their thinking and society as a whole. These ideas also make one look outside of self for power to make things happen, leaving them incapacitated to produce freedom for themselves by re-arranging their thoughts and motion where they do right for the right reason and freeing them to accomplish any idea they embark on.

Traditions are practices or rituals determined by those who came before us that are integral parts of the cultures most of us are part of. Traditions should only be perpetuated if they serve to make us more righteous, which will increase the level of freedom we experience in life. Otherwise they should be discarded or changed to be in harmony with truth or right. Perpetuating a practice that doesn't serve us out of tradition is unwise and will rob us of the freedom we seek.

c) Human Rights
The only right we have is to do right. When we are consistently doing right, the power in right will ensure we are protected so that we can continue performing and magnifying right.

Right is that which can be proven and is in harmony with nature and perpetuates Life and peace. Since everything is a result of thought, to be right, it starts with our thoughts being right. When our thoughts are right, they are factual and in harmony with the laws of nature and what they produce is in agreement with Life or nature.

So when we ask for the freedom to exercise our rights, in essence we are appealing to those whom we perceive as coming in the way of us expressing our purpose in life. Our ultimate purpose is to magnify life and we magnify life by thinking and doing right.

Since we are the masters of our destiny, whatever other people are able to do to or with us is what we permit them. No weapon formed against us can prosper as long as we are living righteously, because all decisions and choices we make and the subsequent circumstances we produce will ensure we are safe and protected to carry on our divine duty of magnifying life. All suffering is a result of wrong thoughts that are in disharmony with the laws of nature or righteousness. Suffering is an indication that we are headed in the wrong direction and should change course. We are to use our uncomfortable circumstances and misfortunes as learning tools to expand our awareness of life and prepare us to make decisions or choices in the future that will enable us to produce only favorable circumstances and conditions in our lives.

When we think and do right, we are exercising our right to live life freely. This means by birthright we are capable of doing and producing things that are right and in our favor and no one or force is powerful enough to stop us from exercising this right.

d) Mass Media and Opinions
The media is an entity controlled by a few people who have taken it upon themselves to determine what the majority should know, believe, think and want. They choose which information is relayed to us and from what perspective. They

also determine the tone and context to use to produce the type of understanding and reaction they want.

Unfortunately most of the reactions and their results are not in favor of the whole nor do they promote freedom. They only serve a few by maintaining their appearance of control over others.

Most of the thoughts and beliefs we think are ours are in fact ideas that were programmed into us by others through repeated exposure. When an idea is constantly repeated, the mind will eventually start to believe it and accept it as truth. A good example is how we all learned to answer to our names after hearing it so many times. Most concepts in movies are the same ideas, like lying, cheating, deception and murder and as a whole we have accepted this as the only reality to expect. In life we get what we expect, and this is a law. So when wars are waged and there is carnage and destruction, we are not as shocked when we see it on TV because it is a reality we expect and the intensity of the situations pale heavily compared to what we have already seen repeatedly in movies and video games.

Some movies show the villains, the bad guys, getting away with their wrong therefore giving the impression to many that crime pays. Those who stand for justice are tortured and murdered and those responsible are depicted getting away with it, so it makes it seem in most people's minds that trying to stand up for what is right is futile.

When news reports share information, most of it is incomplete or non-factual and is shared from the perspective that sympathizes with the ruling class. People are then always left looking at events that are reported in a certain way that is in the favor of those sanctioning this mass mind conditioning. The masses are programmed to think they are powerless and hopelessly dependent on the ruling class to dictate to them how to live their lives. In reality this is so far from the truth. The truth is that we have power to create our own reality by the thoughts we pay attention to and the way we conduct ourselves. The sooner people realize that they have unlimited power and complete control over their lives by conscious positive control of their minds, the sooner they will realize that their ability to be free is entirely up to them.

Movies and TV programs consistently infuse into the minds of the people how to view themselves and the world around them. Most people determine how they will live their lives based on what mass media portrays to them as hip, fashionable and acceptable. Views on ideas like schools, career, spouses, children, friends, fashion, diet, cars, homes, success, happiness etc. are methodically inserted into our minds through movies, music, magazines, commercials etc. The way we look at these aspects of life is very unrealistic however we believe in these notions so strongly that we try to bend reality to fit the fantasies in our heads, to our own detriment. We are trying to emulate the lifestyles we see portrayed on movie and TV screens, unaware that they are illusions.

After constant exposure, people accept these concepts of life, values, tastes and sensibilities as their own which then makes them think, dress, eat and behave a certain way. This makes it very easy for those in power to control the masses as they become heavily dependent on media to share with them what is acceptable and what is not.

Proper use of mass media is to inspire, motivate, and empower people to live their highest visions in peace, love, joy and prosperity. Can you imagine the type of world we will have if all these TV and Radio programs where only transmitting material that makes people more aware of how to conduct themselves intelligently, positively, harmoniously, peacefully etc.?

To control your own thoughts, you have to think factually. A FACT is that which can be proven and is non-personal, meaning it is what it is regardless to how many people agree with or accept it. An opinion is a thought that hasn't been proven or verified with evidence in nature, and once that thought has been proven, then it is now a fact. When we all start basing all our decisions and motion on facts, then most of the problems we face personally and as a world that are results of assumptions, beliefs, opinions, guesses etc. will cease to exist. Everything that is real can be proven in no limit of time. Some things can be proven with physical proof, while others mathematically. We can have opinions on things, however it is unwise to base life-changing decisions on them for the mere fact that we might be in error. In the face of facts, opinions, theories, assumptions, beliefs, guesses etc. should be thrown out of the window. This is why we should constantly study, in order to confirm our thoughts with facts, therefore enabling us to operate based on what is accurate, which greatly increases our chances of success in all we do. Make decisions based on that which can be proven to work. Have the idea of serving the whole, humanity, as the motive behind all you think and do and life will reward you accordingly.

e) Social Class System

We should think about, interact with and treat everyone in a way that makes them see themselves as valuable fractions of the whole, or Life. Everyone is valuable in life, else if they were not, they would not have a purpose therefore would not be in existence. The Creator is not wasteful by having parts of the universe that serve no purpose to the whole. This correct perception of life begins with us viewing ourselves

77

accurately. Since all life has equal purpose, no life is greater or more special than another. An excellent analogy is that of our bodies and the different cells that it is comprised of. Every cell has a purpose and when it is not doing its part the entire body is affected negatively, and vice versa.

When we view ourselves as equally valuable fractions of the whole, we are more apt to treat others the same way. Any imbalance in our perception of ourselves will produce an imbalanced view of others as well. We may try to over-compensate our insecurities and perceived inadequacies by looking down on others and treating them like we are bigger and they are smaller or we are more valuable than them. When we value our connection to the whole, we will value the role of others to us; therefore understand that whatever we do to others we have also done it to ourselves.

When we treat others in a manner that makes them feel small, we stunt their growth and stifle their potential, which equals us robbing the whole, ourselves included, of the benefits of experiencing everyone's natural potential and talents.

When one sees themselves as bigger than others, or more valuable, it produces a tendency for them to think they are above the law, or that the same laws that govern everyone else making sure everything goes right, are beneath them. This produces corrupt habits that lead to chaos and confusion. When corrected, people who view themselves as bigger than others are most likely to reject the correction, so they keep perpetuating the wrong thinking to everyone's detriment. Examples are many, like parents who don't listen to their children when the children are correct. Leaders who don't listen to their followers. Spouses who reject truth from their partners. If they did value others as they value themselves, they would easily accept the correction as if it is coming from them, and reap the benefits of the correction and elevation of thought.

Interestingly when it comes to Mathematics, dealing with numbers, everyone is on the same page and level. Regardless as to how one views themselves and others, they are subject to the same rules, formulas and principles. When dealing with numbers it will be evidently absurd for one to say because they are the king of a vast kingdom therefore the formula 1+1=2 that is used and obeyed by everyone else(his subjects) doesn't apply to them. So when we adopt thinking mathematically/factually, where all our thoughts and decisions are based on mathematical proof by gathering and adding up facts, then all men will have a system to operate on where everyone is equal. Everyone will be able to share an idea and have it accepted or rejected by others based purely on the mathematical proof behind it, without considering the person's popularity, social status, financial well-being etc.

The current world thrives on this class system, the have and have-nots, the knowledgeable and the ignorant, the civilized and the savages, the strong and the weak etc. Instead of the haves, the knowledgeable, the civilized etc. using their power to elevate others to the same level, they often use it to exploit others in order to perpetuate their positions. What they are unaware of is the subtle loneliness and guilt they face which grows and eats away at them every day and eventually destroys them.

f) Corruption

Corruption has become synonymous with bad governance of any entity, especially ruling governments in various countries. Corruption is the motion of doing things contrary to set systems that make sure a given idea goes successfully. When thought is put into establishing a set way to achieve certain goals, then any idea or motion that disrupts or goes against this set way will corrupt the system, producing chaos and confusion. The main reasons why individuals choose to go against a set system agreed upon by the whole to produce results that benefit the whole are greed and selfishness. When one is only interested in personal gain, they ignore the well-being of the whole or other people outside of themselves. This is caused by a flaw in the person's thinking that makes them see themselves as separate from others, thereby they are not seeing the inherent connection we all share that makes everything we think and do affect everyone else. Whatever we do to ourselves we have also done to others, and vice versa. So when we circumvent a system that benefits more than just us, we have shown an unwillingness to do our part to make sure things go right for all, even ourselves, for temporary personal gain. When we do things right based on set systems designed to benefit all then we also benefit as individuals in the long-term by eradicating the possibility of chaos and confusion coming in to disrupt our peace.

A good example to show the effects of corruption is the human body and its many intricate systems that work in harmony for the well-being of the whole body. Every cell of each organ plays a vital part by performing its function diligently as part of a tissue of an organ. When one cell deviates from its set design or purpose, that puts a toll on other cells around it, which in turn affects the whole tissue. This in turn affects the entire organ and eventually the whole body. The effects of the cell might seem negligible on the surface; however it is still registered by the whole body. This understanding of how connected everything is and the effects of minute changes in one area affecting the whole is crucial in understanding how life works and therefore why it is important for all of us to think accurately and perform our motion in accordance with set laws of nature. These laws are here to protect us all.

As intelligent beings we are crucial parts of an intelligent entity known as the universe. When we perform our duty of magnifying peace and life around and within ourselves, this ensures peace and life is magnified in our families, communities, and countries, and also on the planet, solar system, galaxy and eventually the entire universe. Charity begins at home.

It is understandable why most people are frustrated with the current political systems and the so-called leaders. However guess what? These people are products of the same society and system that produced us, which means they are merely expressing the same thinking most of us have. It is just that they are in positions of power that affect more than themselves however the same thinking they are operating on is common among us as a whole. Again, charity begins at home, so when one lies, cheats and steals in their own home with family and friends, they will also lie, cheat and steal when they are in a higher office. If YOU and ME do not correct our thinking so that WE ARE the change we want to see around us, then things will remain the same at best, or get worse. To illustrate this point, look at all the so-called leaders that have campaigned to be presidents and promised positive changes only to turn out to be worse than their predecessor. Until our thinking changes from wrong to right, our conditions will remain the same or get worse. Each of us is not exempt from making this change, so talking about people in power like they are supposed to be oh-so righteous while we remain corrupt ourselves is a waste of our valuable time. Ask yourself, if you were in a position of power, will you institute systems that serve EVERYBODY equally and fairly? Do you deal with everyone equally and fairly right now regardless to their social or economic status? Most of us do not because we have never been taught how to think properly which will enable us to be fair and just to all. The society we came from promotes an unfair class system, the haves and the have-nots, the learned and the unlearned, the royalty and the peasants, etc. So, as long as this corrupt mentality exists, the corruption in all areas of life, including higher offices, will continue.

To eradicate corruption in all its forms, we have to eradicate it in our thinking first by harmonizing our thoughts with the laws of the universe. This will ensure that we only operate on positive thoughts and only do things that produce peace and harmony, not merely for temporary personal gain like it has become the norm in this day and time. Abiding by the laws and principles of nature, and any set rules and systems designed to positively govern our motion will benefit everyone, us included.

Personal Experiences

I understood at the onset of my quest to finding the meaning of life that what I was taught was not anything to go by, and that I needed the ability to discern what is true from falsehood on my own. I made up my mind that I had to be open to all knowledge and then utilize my reasoning power to determine what was true or false. Even though I was raised in a Christian family, I knew Christianity did not have all the answers I needed, because if it did, I would have figured out the answers to my questions myself after all those years of going to church, bible studies and attending a Christian boarding school. I wanted a system of thinking that will enable me to know right from wrong, real from unreal, good from bad, beneficial from harmful etc. That want was answered in the form of (formulas of accurate thinking) mathematical thinking classes which were taught as the foundation of a personal and community development curriculum which formed the core of a community rebuilding program I participated in for close to a decade. These classes and the way of thinking they instilled in the participants allowed me to start seeing reality for what it really is, based on facts. This prepared me to make sound decisions that are in harmony with the past, present and future. It took practice to control my emotions and the ego when getting corrected when I erred in my calculations of my day to day motion. This practice is ongoing, and the more I exercise this control, the better I get at it. For example, it took practice for me to be able to have someone bring to my attention something I did in error that I needed to correct. Thoughts like "who does this person think he is?", "I don't have to listen to this", "You are not perfect either", "What I did was justified", and the list goes on, came to mind. I know these thoughts come from the negative force trying to coerce me to ignore the Truth of the situation and use my own power of thinking and energy to defend it (negative force) by defending the wrong I did. Now my focus is on what works, therefore I am open to accept the lesson or what is beneficial or the Truth or right from everything and everyone, especially in people and situations. The ability to accept correction regardless to whom it is coming from should be a core subject taught in all schools in order to produce progressively peaceful, intelligent, efficient and productive citizens of the world. Being humble enough to learn from others has allowed me to gain different and beneficial insights into various areas of life, which has empowered me to make choices that have resulted in tremendous growth in my understanding of myself and the world around me. I now better understand the forces that control world economics, religion and politics, mass consciousness and behavior, trade and commerce. I also have an understanding based on scientific, mathematical and experiential evidence that the only way for me to be free to do, have and become anything I want in life regardless to what is going on in the world is by staying positive in my thoughts and actions. The negative force is always whispering something to make me miss the right or truth in a situation so that I bring in failure, chaos and confusion in my experiences. The technique that works best for me is finding something I am grateful for in my life each time I find myself thinking a negative thought. Gratitude is a high vibrational positive emotion, and low vibrational emotions are dissipated or automatically disappear when one is in a high vibration. I also constantly remind myself that there is always something for me to learn in every situation and from every person. All these are skills I am now aware of and still mastering, and each day I get better at it.

Chapter 3 – The Physical

1. Proper Action

In this chapter we are going to explore actions one can take to increase the degree of freedom they experience in their life. Knowing is not enough, we have to move out and apply what we know to get the results we want. Mere thoughts count for nothing unless carried into action.

A. Self-Discipline

It is important for us to exercise self-discipline by ignoring the negative voice in our head that is always whispering suggestions to take us off course to reaching our goals. The worst negative habit that keeps most in bondage of failure is laziness. Laziness is when we lie around doing nothing knowing very well there is something we are supposed to be doing, in other words, not being in motion unjustifiably so. Successful people have developed a habit of doing what needs to be done regardless to whether they like to do it or not. We have to discipline ourselves to stay in motion working towards our goals especially when we feel like not doing anything. Laziness breeds many more negative habits like lying as people try to justify why they did not do something, cheating as people try to compensate for their lack of work or effort etc. We can easily free ourselves from these negative habits by exercising self-discipline, which is simply the ability to do what we told ourselves we are going to do. It is easier to discipline self when the purpose of what we are doing remains at the fore front of our minds.

B. Constant Study

The more we are aware of, the more we can do and become. The more we can do and become, the more freedom we have. In other words, the more our awareness grows, the more elevated our thoughts and living conditions are, therefore the more life within us we are able to express without restrictions, thereby making us more free. So, to grow and elevate in our thinking, we have to continually study new concepts that make life work better for us. We should develop a love for truth, and an insatiable appetite for knowledge that we can apply to ourselves for continuous growth in our thinking and behavior. We are living at a very exciting time when vast knowledge about any subject under the sun is readily available to the common man due to the affordable internet access as well as mobile technology. Knowledge that was once only privileged to the rich and powerful about how life works and how to develop ourselves into the free and prosperous human beings we were designed to be is now available to all, almost free of charge. The duty is now on every individual to develop the will to know better and do better with their life by seeking out the knowledge to make their dreams a reality. On the reverse side, as more knowledge is available, the negative force has also made sure there are equally, if not more distractions to take people's minds away from real life using the same technology. For the majority, they are using technology to distract and disempower themselves instead of using it as a tool for empowerment. There are full grown able-bodied people who squander entire days playing violent video games that are poisoning their minds instead of learning new skills and insights by listening to or watching positive material that will make them better, more successful and happier people.

Since we now know better just by being exposed to the ideas in this book, we are going to continue to study and feed our minds with ideas that are beneficial to achieving our goals and realizing the life of our dreams. There are a lot of self-development books, as well as audio and video programs out there covering all areas of life. It is better to spend our free time saturating our minds with concepts that make us see life more clearly and enable us to control and focus our thoughts better so that we can achieve more using the least amount of time and energy. Instead of listening for an hour to some meaningless music, listen to a self-help audiobook that adds to you. Instead of watching a movie filled with negative images, watch a documentary that expands your awareness. The more aware we are, the more life we can express and the more freedom we are able to experience.

C. Setting Goals

We discussed earlier the need for us to find our purpose in life, that thing we love doing that brings us great joy and makes life more comfortable and pleasurable for others. When we find our purpose, we have to develop a vision on how to fulfill that purpose. To accomplish that vision we have to set short-term goals which are steps to realizing our vision or plan for life. Goals are what guide what we do each and every day. Without a goal, we are like a ship on the ocean without a rudder. We become prone to being taken anywhere because we are at the mercy of the unpredictable currents of the water. Goals enable us to achieve our vision, and our vision is how we fulfill our life's purpose. Our purpose is the reason why we are on the planet right now. Without goals we will live a life of little to no meaningful accomplishment and be a slave working to achieve other people's dreams instead of working to achieve our own dreams. So it is important that we decide what we want to do and become in life, and then outline the steps we are going to need to take to get to that destination. This way we have a point to focus our energy on and it gives everything we do purpose and gives meaning to our existence. Having goals with deadlines enables us to stay focused on what works in bringing about our ideal life, by avoiding anything or anyone that opposes the realization of our dream. For example if you are focused on getting somewhere at a certain time, you will only be able to entertain those going in the same direction and travelling at the same speed, everyone and everything else will have to wait lest it takes you off track. We are much happier when we have goals and as we achieve these goals, our self-esteem and confidence grows and our ability to achieve even greater goals increases.

To assist with achieving goals efficiently, we are going to discuss a few keys to success. Most of us get overwhelmed easily when they have to deal with more than one task or goal at a time in pursuit of their vision. We often find ourselves trying to tackle everything at the same time, utilizing what is called multi-tasking. The mind can only focus on one idea at a time, so multi-tasking does not really work the way we think it does. We can have multiple tasks running at the same time however our mind can only focus on one task at a time. This is where the ability to manage motion or activities comes in. Whatever tasks we plan to accomplish, it is highly recommended to write them down in the order of importance, not ease, preferably the night before. This gives our minds time to go over ways to accomplish these tasks successfully as we rest. Also when we get up we are already focused because we know what needs to be completed and in what order, which will cut back on the length of time it will take to get things done.

Focus on one task at a time and only deal with that one task until it is completed before you move to the next one. This will eliminate distractions that easily take people off course. The more focused one is on one task at a time, the greater their chances of completing it successfully in a timely fashion because all their attention and energy is going into that one task. This is also why to be successful in achieving the life of your dreams, you have to set specific goals based on importance and then go forth to accomplish that one top priority goal first. This helps by ensuring your time and energy are utilized in a more concentrated way to achieve the most success in the least amount of time and opens the door for more successes since one success leads to more successes. When we try to tackle a lot of tasks or goals at the same time, we spread our time and energy out and will most likely not achieve much. There is an old saying that he who chases two cats will catch neither. Spreading our energy over a lot of tasks or goals will lessen focus on any given task or goal thereby reducing attention which leads to less effort and greater possibility of failure. Another way to look at it is viewing your goals or tasks as seeds and your time and energy as water. If you plant too many seeds at a time, and then try to water them at the same time, you will run out of water before any of the seeds grow. However if you focus your attention on one or two seeds, you will be able to give the required attention and have enough water for them to grow and bear fruit and make it possible for you to grow more seeds in the future. Find that one goal that when it is realized will open up more channels for you to accomplish more goals in pursuit of your vision. This could be a book that when finished will enable you to pursue doing a movie or TV series. This approach to completing goals will make it possible for us to achieve greatly in the least amount of time utilizing minimum energy.

The last yet very important key to being successful at accomplishing anything meaningful in life is persistence. As children we express a very high degree of persistence and that ability is taken from us we grow from the way adults around us respond to us. All great men and women of the past shared this common trait of being persistent until they realized the fruits of their labor. This means whatever we have in our mind to do, we have to commit our time and energy to its completion regardless to how many obstacles we encounter. We should be quick to act and very slow to quit, if ever. There are stories of men who started digging for gold and because of impatience and lack of persistence; they abandoned the mine when they did not run into the vein of gold. Surprisingly somebody came along, bought the mine and dug just a few feet more and ran into a fortune in gold. This is a profound lesson to illustrate the importance of perseverance in all we do.

As we grow in our ability to accomplish ideas successfully and efficiently, we experience more freedom.

D. Positive Relationships
It is important that we always keep around us people who are in support of our dreams, lest they become the barrier between us and our freedom. We are truly free when we are able to realize all our dreams, and anyone who comes against our dreams is against us becoming ourselves, which equates to them being against us being free. We are to surround ourselves with like thinking minds, positive and ambitious people who also believe in their dreams as much as they believe in ours. It has been said, and it is true, that association brings about assimilation. We end up adopting the traits and habits of the people we associate with the most. If they are positive and about progress, the same qualities will rub off onto us and vice versa. To reach higher

and accomplish greatly, we have to associate with people who are not prone to being used by the negative force to come against us to cancel out our noble ideas. The negative force can accomplish this through others sharing discouraging comments like "you can't do it", or displaying unsupportive behavior like smoking in front of you when you are trying to quit smoking or similar negative influences.

Also remember, everything and everyone in our lives we attracted to ourselves based on our dominant thought patterns. Most times we focus on what we do not want in people and relationships, and we end up getting more of the same. To attract a certain type of relationship, be it a friend, business partner, wife or husband, we first have to know exactly what we want and why. We have the power to dictate what type of person or relationship we will bring into our reality. We achieve this by imagining the person we want, their traits and the experiences we will have with them. When we constantly imagine how it will feel being with this person or having this relationship, with faith that we shall receive this reality and being deeply grateful for it, then this person or relationship will walk into our life. The more we expect this person or relationship, the better for us because we will start noticing all the opportunities to bring this reality about. Nothing ventured, nothing gained, so try it and see the results in your own life!

E. Fast Action

Once we have set our goals and outlined the tasks that have to be completed to reach those goals, we need to take fast action to complete them. Most times we procrastinate or spend inordinate amounts of time planning and re-planning how to accomplish a task towards our goal. The best way to learn how to do a thing is to actually move out and do it. If you are planning to write a book, start today. Do an outline, and start filling in the details as much and as soon as the ideas come to your mind. Do something towards your goal every day. Every little bit counts. Delaying action leads to unnecessary suffering. Most times we dread the action needed to get to our goal especially if it is something we have not done before. We imagine it is going to be difficult instead of imagining it being easy and fun. So, next time you plan to do something, instead of dreading how difficult it is going to be, just take fast action and do it. If it really is that difficult, it is better to experience the difficulty while in motion instead of suffering twice, first in your mind and then when you are actually doing it. Usually, once in motion, a better way to accomplish the task will furnish itself and you will discover it was not difficult at all. Fast action will remove unnecessary delays to reaching your goals by building your momentum, confidence, and providing crucial feedback on what adjustments need to be made to improve efficiency and accuracy.

F. Asking for Help

This is one habit that will make a world of difference to the level of success we experience in life in our quest to be free. Most people do everything else to succeed at reaching their goals but ask for help when the situation calls for it. We avoid asking for help because we are fearful of rejection. However when we really look at it, how worse can rejection be? Our situation is still the same when we do not ask as it is when we get a rejection, and things will only change when we ask and get the help. If we do not ask for help, the answer will always be no. When someone we ask for help is unavailable or not interested in helping, there is always somebody else to step up to accomplish the task. Being able to ask for help takes understanding that it is better to ask and get a rejection than to keep quite and never know if we could have received the help we wanted. Failing to reach a goal because we did not ask for help when we clearly saw we needed it will have us live with regret. What if we asked for the help and received it? How would the help have changed the outcome? So it is important to know when to ask for help and actually have the courage to approach those who can help to see if they can assist. We are put on the planet to work together, and most people feel their worth most when they are assisting others reach their goals. It adds a sense of accomplishment to their lives. Remember this, it is the wheel that squeaks that gets the oil and closed mouths do not get fed.

G. Drive for Improvement

We should always be looking to improve everything about ourselves, as well as things and situations we interact with. The common tendency of the masses is to merely maintain things as they are. This is why we have clichés like if it is not broken do not fix it. Just because it is not broken does not mean it is right and cannot or should not be improved upon. We have been programmed to settle for how things are and rarely explore ways to make them better, especially ourselves, our thoughts and behavior.

Constantly observe yourself, your interactions with everyone and everything and take note of things about yourself that need refinement or improvement to make those interactions much smoother and more harmonious. By having a constant drive for improvement and not merely waiting until things go wrong to fix them, you will start noticing opportunities for growth in everything by looking at how things could be made to run better. This way of thinking brings a more exciting dynamic to life which adds greatly to our level of freedom as we constantly elevate to levels of existence that are immune to negative.

H. Imagination

Now that we understand that everything is a result of thought, and thoughts are actually things that will take form as objects and experiences in our physical world, it is paramount that we practice holding the thoughts of what we want to see and experience in our minds. This is a process called imagination, the motion of holding and experiencing images in our minds, as if they already exist. Thoughts are processed as images in our minds. Whatever we describe or think about, we see a picture of it in the mind's eye. Because we want to experience a life of success, happiness and freedom, we have to diligently practice holding images in our minds that will produce results that match the life we want. This means always thinking about what we want to see and experience, especially in the face of situations that are unfavorable.

When we worry we are utilizing our power of imagination to paint pictures of things we do not want to see or experience. The images we hold will generate emotions in us, the emotions will motivate us to act, and our actions will produce the results that match the image. We should practice holding positive images in our minds by always looking for the positive in things, people and situations and constantly magnifying that. We should look to see what we can do, or think of everything that can go right in a situation, or how we would like things to turn out in our lives. We should employ our faculty of imagination to paint vivid pictures of these things and experiences we want in our lives, and actually expect them. We attract what we expect, and we expect what we imagine. Always imagine reaching and already experiencing your goals, especially during your leisure time. Remember this, whatever we imagine, it exists. Thoughts are real in the spiritual world, so whatever you are creating in your mind, it already exists in the unseen and is now just waiting to take form in the physical world. Let us utilize our imagination for our benefit and the benefit of the entire world.

I. Communication is Key

In all we do, at the base of it are relationships and purposes served. This entails communication of ideas to somebody else, even if it is just ourselves. This has to be done in a way that ensures the idea is clearly understood and then completed efficiently and precisely. When we communicate clearly and timely with all we are interacting with in any endeavor in Life, be it a relationship, business partnership etc., we give everyone enough time and details of what happened, is happening or is going to happen, when, by whom and everything else required to make the idea successful. So if the person/people we are communicating with would like to assist, they may do so, or if they have a better recommendation on how to make things work more smoothly, they have an opportunity to share it.

Applying this principle of communicating consistently will greatly increase our chances of success in whatever we do. For example, suppose we live in a home with others and we decide to renovate one part of the home and we hire a contractor to finish the job over the weekend. This motion will affect everyone in the home, and if there is no communication on our part about what is going to be happening and why, we might unnecessarily inconvenience others by having no access to that part of the home, or if it requires turning off one of the utilities, then others are ill-prepared to deal with that event. If we, however communicate with everyone in detail and in a timely manner what we are planning, then others have an opportunity to prepare for any interruption in utilities, or lack of access to that part of the home. Furthermore, if they have a better recommendation regarding the work about to take place or know an even better contractor to finish the job on time at a more reasonable price, then they are able to express it.

Lack of proper communication opens the door for confusion and friction to come in. Most times when we do not communicate properly, we leave others with only assumptions to go by, especially if they do not come to us to check and get all the facts regarding an idea or motion. The negative force in each of us thrives on this lack of communication and uses it to throw wrenches into motion, usually through somebody who was not properly informed about the motion, and who operates comfortably on assumptions. For example, suppose we have a vehicle we share with others, and we have some work done to the brakes however did not get it completed and we do not communicate with others about this potential hazard. When somebody in the home utilizes the car and does not do any prior checking to make sure everything is functioning properly, a door is left open for a negative experience and harm to occur. This can easily be avoided when proper communication and checking takes place. It is better to over communicate than withholding information from people who need it. It is better to have information and not need it than not to have it and then need it.

J. Properly Considering Everything and Prioritizing

To be successful in any endeavor we are about to embark on, we have to gather as much facts as possible about the situation and intelligently prioritize them to make sure our decisions regarding the motion are accurate. The more facts we consider and properly prioritize, the greater the possibility of reaching a more accurate decision or the outcome we want. The facts that we leave out coupled with improper prioritizing will be the measure of our level of failure as these are doors left open through which friction can enter.

For example, suppose we plan to leave somebody watching over our house over the weekend and we want them to be comfortable as well as have the house in the same condition we left it. The more we consider, and the more detailed and encompassing our instructions are, the more likelihood that we will achieve the results we want. If we leave out a few facts about certain aspects of the home that need to be paid attention to as well as fail to point out what takes priority over what, the greater the possibility of something undesirable taking place.

K. Dealing with First Transgression

Whenever we encounter a scenario in life, to solve it most efficiently, we have to pin-point the first instance that the laws that make things work right were transgressed. This approach ensures we get to the root of what produced the scenario and resolve it in a way that properly addresses everything else that is wrong that might have taken place as a result of this first transgression. Most times people try to solve the after effects of a problem which is impossible to do when the first transgression has not been identified and corrected.

For example, one is having some serious skin problems and they are trying all sorts of creams to get rid of the skin irritations however nothing seem to be working. Since they understand that we are what we eat, they decide to analyze their diet to see which foods they are eating that is causing the skin irritations. They then start eliminating certain foods until they get to the real culprit. This food is the first transgression. In another example you have a friend visit another without letting them know they are coming because they want to surprise them. When they get to their house they find the door locked and after calling them they discover their friend is out of town visiting their relatives for a few days. Now, this situation could have been avoided had the friend done the right thing, which is call and check with his friend if he is going to be in town and if he can visit. Not calling to check is the first transgression, and if that was addressed, all the other inconveniences would not have taken place.

L. Don't Take It Personal

After understanding that everything is an expression of either the positive force or the reaction to it, negative, it brings a new awareness to how we handle other people. Nothing that anyone does should be taken personally, even when it seems they deliberately planned to do it, because at the end of the day, they are merely a tool that is being used by the negative force to produce pain, suffering, chaos and confusion in other people's lives.

When we understand that we are either expressing the positive or negative in us, then we look at what others do as just that, an expression of the positive creative force or the negative destructive force. There really is no in between where we can say this is me or that is you. It is always either of these two forces. The best we can do when somebody does something negative to us, is to use that situation or experience to our advantage. By learning the lesson and what we need to do next time, we can prevent being vulnerable again. There is a lesson in every experience, even if it is just to learn how it feels going through that experience so that we can explain it to somebody else later in life. We lose a lot of time and energy replaying in our minds how bad somebody treated us or how bad things went instead of looking at the lesson in it and preparing ourselves to avoid a similar situation from happening again.

What others do or say to us and how they treat us is merely a reflection of their understanding of themselves, or lack thereof, and their level of mastery of the two natures within. When they do or say positive things to us, that reflects their ability to think positively and having better control of their negative nature. The opposite is true when others treat us negatively, it is a reflection of their lack of control of their negative nature. What we can do is try to help them by reminding them of their positive nature and accentuating it, by sharing with them what would be the best way to treat others and why. If they are unable to check their negative nature and are unwilling to accept our recommendations, then we can remove ourselves from them until they grow and develop to the point where their thinking and behavior does not offend us anymore.

In reality all people caught up in negative thoughts and behavior deserve our compassion, especially when we understand the forces at play which is causing them to think and act the way they do. In some cases disagreeable behavior by others is simply a cry for help. They need assistance to get back on the right path. Operating from this understanding will free us from negative emotions like anger, hate, resentment, disappointment etc. that usually come up when we take things that happen to us personally.

When we look at ourselves in a non-personal way as mere expressions of the positive or negative forces, we will free ourselves from guilt and shame much easier. When we do something in error and we realize it, the intelligent thing to do is to realize that we allowed our thinking to be hijacked by the negative force and we need to correct ourselves immediately. We do this by identifying the negative thought that produced the unfavorable scenario and replace it with the opposite and positive thought. To solidify this positive thought into our thinking we have to create activities around it that enable us to apply that positive thought repeatedly until it becomes part of our everyday thinking. When this is done, our focus is now on the positive or lesson from the situation, therefore freeing us from feeling guilt and shame.

I. Diet and Exercise

It is a well-known fact that we are what we eat. This principle applies to all levels of existence; spiritual, mental and physical. The ideas we feed our minds will determine the type of thoughts and activities we will engage in and also how we treat everything and everyone, mainly our own bodies. When one thinks right and positively, they will involve themselves in righteous and positive activities as well as treat everything right, starting with their body. Proper treatment of the body starts with feeding it the healthiest foods one can find. In reality our bodies are where we live so we have to treat them right if we intend to be comfortable in them. What right thinking person wants to stay in a dirty and uncomfortable home?

Our health is our wealth. Health cannot be bought; it has to be earned by constantly applying knowledge of healthy living. The knowledge and discipline needed to maintain a healthy body comes from a healthy mind. A healthy mind is one with ideas that are always geared to promote life and peace.

Since everything is rooted in thought, so is health and disease. Healthy thoughts promote healthy habits, which produce a healthy body. Negative thoughts turn into negative habits which in turn produce an unhealthy body. Thought is energy and negative thoughts make the body susceptible to disease which thrives in negative low-vibrational environments. Another way to look at it is that energy creates or begets like energy. Negative thoughts are negative energy and will create or attract more negative energy to it. Disease is a manifestation of negative energy in the body.

Most of the ideas already covered about how to think and look at things right or positively constitute a healthy diet for our minds. Other aspects of a healthy diet that need further analysis are the mental and physical ones. Mental activities that promote mental health include puzzles, solving mathematical problems, watching movies that involve reasoning and expanding our awareness of things around us, like documentaries. On the physical aspect, our bodies are intricate masterpieces that require great care in how we feed, clean, exercise and rest them. Our bodies are sophisticated pieces of machinery capable of doing many things. However for the majority of us we are missing the operator's manual for these machines, so we are unaware of their many functions and maintenance procedures.

First and foremost, our bodies are primarily composed of water so drinking plenty of clean water regularly is essential to a healthy body. It helps with regulating the body's metabolism and processes as well as flushing out toxins among many other things.

Secondly, since we are what we eat, the more live foods we intake, the more life we put into our bodies and the healthier we are. Fruits and vegetables should constitute the majority of our foods. When we eat filth or animals that eat filth, like scavenging animals, our bodies will also reflect that.

Thirdly, proper elimination of waste from the body is crucial to the overall health of a person. Normally, we should have at least one elimination (bowel movement) everyday if we eat every day, ideally 2 or so hours after a meal. The sooner our bodies eliminate waste, the less opportunity the waste has to negatively affect our body functions causing disease. The cleaner our digestive track is, mainly the colon or large intestine where the waste gathers before being expelled from the body, the healthier we are. Lack of proper elimination of bowels causes fecal matter to collect in the colon and then putrefy and create conditions for unhealthy organisms to grow and is the root cause of colon cancer. It also affects our thinking abilities and the level of energy we express. Eating a lot of fruits and vegetables assists greatly in maintaining a healthy colon, by providing roughage or fiber, which ensures we have easy regular eliminations of waste. Proper water intake keeps our bowels loose and moist for easy expelling of fecal matter and decreases the likelihood of being constipated and having gas.

Fourth, our bodies are designed to move and for each muscle we use regularly, the healthier that muscle is and the stronger the body becomes. The saying that if you do not use it you lose it also applies to our bodies. When we neglect utilizing certain muscles, they start wasting away. Exercise and stretching ensures we keep most of, if not all of our muscles in shape and good condition so that whenever we need to use them, they are ready. Our bodies are designed to stand and move a certain way, and the muscles work together to maintain our posture and balance. When some muscles are used and others are neglected, an imbalance occurs to the entire body and sooner or later these imbalances will take a toll and manifest in structural issues that cause chronic aches and pains.

Lastly, because of the constant wear and tear that takes place to our bodies while we are in motion, rest is a must to enable the body to heal and repair.

Below are a few practices to adopt to enhance your diet:

For seven days, drink half your body weight in ounces of water throughout the day. For example if you weigh 120lbs, drink 60 ounces of water throughout the day, for at least seven days. You will notice your body has more energy, you are much calmer, you will have more and easier bowel movements and skin issues will start to get better apart from other benefits.

For seven days, eat fruits for breakfast and snack and have more salad and vegetable dishes for dinner with little to no meat, especially red meat. You will notice immediate changes like more energy, wounds healing faster, easy bowel movements etc.

For seven days, exercise regularly and if permissible for 1 hour each day doing pushups, sit-ups, walking, swimming, running and stretching. The benefits will range from more energy, healthier appetite, more strength, to more regular sleep patterns.

For rest, take 10-15 minute naps during the day when permissible. This will help rejuvenate your body and enable you to focus. Get at least 6 solid hours of sleep 2 hours after having a meal to ensure your body properly shuts down and have enough time to repair.

J. Proper Food Production

Out of all man's needs and wants, the first and most basic one is food. When we are born, the first thing we cry out for is milk, food, signifying its importance to physical life. It is food that keeps us here or takes us away depending on how nutritious or poisonous the food is to our bodies. Food comes from the earth and the health of the soil determines the value and quality of our food, which in turn determines our health. Remember, we are what we eat. A healthy soil will produce healthy and nutritious food, which will also produce healthy people since our bodies are built from the components of the earth that comes through our food.

For us to be healthy and energetic, we have to eat the right foods farmed naturally from a healthy soil full of life. Most foods we consume today are either genetically modified or grown using unnatural chemical fertilizers or both. These foods lack proper nutrients and life force from the earth. Chemical fertilizers used in monoculture farming leave the soil lifeless and unbalanced because they kill the essential microorganisms that give the soil life and nutrients, like earthworms and other microbes.

The more chemical fertilizers we use, the more barren the soil becomes and the more dependent on these chemical fertilizers we become, and the less nutritious the food becomes. Earthworms and other microbes keep the soil rich in nutrients, trace minerals and humus by breaking down organic matter which is where the plants get their nutrients from and in turn give them to animals. Without these earthworms and microbes, the cycle in nature that converts organic matter into nutrients is drastically affected, which in turn affects many other cycles in the ecosystem, especially man's health.

Proper farming methods are a critical key in healing the people through healing the soil. By adopting natural and sustainable methods like composting, mulching and permaculture, we can begin restoring the health of the soil. Composting helps in breaking down organic matter into easily absorbed nutrients for crops. Mulching reduces the loss of soil moisture through evaporation. This keeps the soil conditions conducive for earthworms and microbes as well as plants. Mulching also reduces soil erosion and controls weeds which greatly reduces the need to cultivate or spray the weeds, leaving the soil's integrity intact. Permaculture is the growing of plants for fruits, vegetables, grains, herbs etc. in a system that mimics a forest, which is a balanced ecosystem. It is a farming system void of the negatives of monoculture. With permaculture, because the system is based on the continual growth and balance of the soil, with time the soil fertility gets high, the nutritional value of the food increases as more microbes grow and more organic matter is turned into healthy humus that makes up the top soil.

K. Water Harvesting

Water Harvesting is the collection of run-off water to use domestically and for providing crops with moisture. This is done by collecting rainwater from rooftops and storing it in containers or by channeling runoff water on a terrain or catchment area and directing it into a dam or swell system. This allows for water that will otherwise just runoff causing flooding and soil erosion be stored for future use during times of less water supply, therefore allowing farming to continue unhindered by water shortage.

L. Gardening

Home gardening in urban areas is a practice that can provide a lot of food to reduce the cost of living, dependency on outside sources for food in an unpredictable society, and gives one control over their food and what goes into it. Most vegetables we get from stores are doused in toxic chemicals like pesticides and preservatives. Growing our own food like vegetables and herbs is easy, and doesn't take any more time than we put in making sure our lawns and flowers are maintained, except we eat the vegetables and herbs. Food can easily be grown in plant pots and trays in and around the house, providing a constant supply of food throughout the year. Most of what we do in life is to put food on our tables, which puts us at the mercy of those controlling our food supplies. When we grow our own food, we take control of a big portion of our lives by not having to work excessively just to afford buying food from somebody else. This frees up a lot of our time, which allows us to enjoy increased freedom and independence to pursue other things in life that are of interest to us, making us much happier in addition to the benefit of improved health.

M. Tree Planting

Almost all of us eat and love fruits, right? Imagine the world we can create starting right now by growing trees from the seeds of fruits we eat everyday like avocados, oranges, lemons, apples, mangoes etc. and planting them all over the place, like in our backyards, parks, hills and valleys etc. A Chinese proverb says 'The best time to plant an apple tree was 10 years ago and the next best time is right now". When we all do this simple yet rewarding task, we will have lots of fruit trees producing plentiful food and oxygen for us all, beautifying the landscape, providing us shade and sheltering beautiful birds, insects and other animals. I started this tree-growing project and effortlessly yet successfully produced several tree seedlings for avocado, lemon, orange, grapefruit and apple trees. I will be growing and planting fruit trees wherever there is space all the days of my life and I strongly recommend we all do the same. We can each plant several trees a year. This is one sure way for YOU and ME to leave a lasting positive impression on the planet. It is very easy, fun, therapeutic and immensely gratifying. Let's DO it!

N. Food Processing and Preservation

Another aspect of food which needs exploration is processing and preservation. To ensure we properly use all the food we produce and intelligently store away the remainder for future use, we need to know how to process and preserve foods through methods like canning, freezing and drying.

When people are well fed, they are healthier, happier and have more time and energy to explore other ideas that will increase their level of comfort. When our minds are free from thinking about where the next meal is going to come from, we have ample time to utilize our creative abilities to improve our living conditions by advancing ideas in areas like clothing, shelter, transportation, communication, energy etc.

Our food is our life. How it is produced, stored and processed is our responsibility. It is important that we have a system to secure and feed ourselves the healthiest foods available. We should do more research on the right foods and the best ways to feed ourselves because food is the foundation for our freedom on the physical plane of existence.

O. Civilization

A civilization is a collection of systems that govern the motion of a people in their pursuit to attain a happy and fulfilling existence. At the core of a civilization is man and his interactions with others and everything else in existence. A civilized man is one who treats and interacts with everyone and everything properly according to the purpose and design or nature of said person, place or thing.

When we think of, speak of and interact with people by magnifying their strengths, we will have harmonious relationships. Life is about ideas and their accomplishment.

107

All our interactions with others are to get things done or maintain what is already in motion. This requires the strengths or positive expressions of people. When we keep these positive traits of people at the forefront of our minds and magnify them when dealing with others we produce an environment of success, where people are motivated and free to express their strengths in the accomplishment of ideas.

This principle also applies when dealing with other things. When we treat things according to their purpose or design, we will experience harmony and freedom as we work with said thing to complete ideas. When we treat a vehicle right, keeping it oiled, greased, with good tires, engine properly tuned etc., it will drive well for longer with little to no issues, therefore increasing the level of harmony and freedom we experience while utilizing it. The more we mistreat, neglect and use it outside of its purpose, the more issues, disharmony and friction we will experience.

Here are some examples of the attributes or traits of a civilized person:

They utilize language to promote positive by saying what they like, love, want or what they are in harmony with and willing to do to accomplish ideas. They speak to the positive or lesson of any given situation and also magnify the positive in people or things. As an exercise to develop these traits, regardless to what is being shared or shown to us, we are to look for what is true and helpful. This is easy to see if we ask the question WHY and look for what we can gain from the given situation, thing or person.

Also when interacting with people, we are to share with them what we like, can do and are willing to do in whatever is being asked or presented to us. This type of communication opens doors of opportunities for growth and promotes positive forward motion. We are to refrain from saying No, Can't, Won't, Don't etc. as this stops ideas and removes opportunities for growth through new experiences. We are to share with others what they can do instead of what they can't do. Sharing with someone to stop doing something does not tell them what they should do instead. For example, when we share with a child to stop running in the house, that doesn't share with the child what they need to do, which is walk. So the proper way to express the idea will be to simply share with the child to walk instead of saying don't run. When we focus on the positive, or what can happen, or is possible etc., we produce harmony and promote progress. Posturing oneself to always say yes opens up a lot of doors or opportunities to learn and grow. Since life is about learning and growing through experiences, the more one says yes, the more they will be involved in activities that will expand their awareness through life experiences. Experience is indeed the best teacher.

Civilized people always leave things and situations in the same condition or better than they found them. This takes discipline. Whenever we utilize something, we are to leave it in the same condition or better than when we found it. When we get involved in activities we are to insert ourselves to see what needs to be improved upon and what we can do to make those improvements.

As we utilize everything for the purpose it was intended for, we will notice how much longer it will last and how much freedom we will experience in our interactions with everything. For example a chair is to sit on and should not be used as a stepping stool. When we use it outside of its design, we open up room for misuse and or damage to occur. Standing on a chair puts more weight on it than it is designed to carry. It also has the possibility of damaging the top material on it which is meant to be sat on and not stood on, not to mention the risk of someone falling off it and getting injured. All this can be avoided by simply utilizing everything for the purpose it was designed for.

When it comes to our attire, we should dress properly for the occasion. This gives us the freedom to move and be comfortable participating in any activity without our clothing or lack thereof getting in the way. Being properly dressed boosts our confidence as well as raises our self-esteem.

Our level of civilization is also determined by how well we treat our homes. Doors in homes are designed to be opened and closed gently and quietly by turning the knob, push door open, then turn the other knob, hold it, close the door quietly and then release the knob gently. The door will last longer and the entire environment will be more peaceful. Slamming doors damages the door and frame as well as affects other structural components of the building not to mention creating a non-peaceful environment from all the noise.

Civilized people are mindful of waste and therefore use things intelligently. This includes putting a small amount of toothpaste on a toothbrush, maybe a quarter way of the length of the toothbrush instead of the entire length. Most of the toothpaste that we are accustomed to putting on the entire length of the toothbrush ends up being spate out into the sink and goes down the drain. Only a little amount is needed to actually clean the teeth. We should only run the water when we are wetting the toothbrush and when we are rinsing our mouths and toothbrush. Some just run the water into the drain while brushing the teeth, producing waste. The same idea of conserving water goes for taking showers. We should run the water to wet and lather up our bodies, turn the water off, wash and scrub entire body, then turn the water back on to rinse. We should also turn off lights in rooms that are not being utilized.

Once one starts applying these few simple examples of conserving energy and resources, they will start noticing more opportunities to conserve more, especially their own energy. For example one will start being more calculating in their motion i.e. when one goes to one room downstairs, they should consider everything they need from that room and level before rushing back upstairs to minimize the number of trips up and down as this will eventually wear down most stairways through repeatedly running over them. Same applies to going into the refrigerator to get something, we are to know everything we need from it before opening it so that we don't keep the door open while deciding what we want thereby letting the chill out which will make the fridge work harder to cool everything back down again.

Civilized people are also clean, inwardly and outwardly. One way to keep our homes clean is not to allow filth into the home by taking shoes off at the doorway. This prevents the dirt and filth from outside from being brought and dragged throughout the entire home. A clean home will produce a healthy environment that keeps those who dwell in it healthy.

Order in the house is part of being civilized, meaning having a place and purpose for everything. When things don't have a purpose nor a place, that produces chaos, which leads to stress, inefficiency and unhappiness. With order, motion around the home is efficient because time is not wasted looking for something and the peace of knowing where everything is reduces the possibility of stress and unhappiness. It can easily be frustrating trying to look for something in a cluttered and chaotic environment.

Being civilized equals being righteous, intelligent, harmonious, peaceful and free.

2. Pursuit of Happiness

Our discussion of freedom will not be complete without exploring the idea of happiness. Can one be truly free without happiness? Absolutely not, by the mere fact that not being happy means one is experiencing misery, which is a negative emotion. Happiness is an integral part of life, and is what propels us to seek the things we seek. Life is the constant pursuit of happiness. We pursue things that we think will make us happy. Happiness is an experience that shows one things that are important to them, in a positive manner. This is a state of mind, and is relative to the thinking of the person to whom it is applied. What makes one person happy doesn't necessarily make another person happy, however the formula for happiness is the same for all. It is a product of enjoying and appreciating what one has. Being happy comes from within and the shortest path to being happy is being grateful for everything one has. The greatest thing we all should be grateful for is Life itself. Life is an activity that inspires us to enjoy the present with great anticipation of the future. We experience Life when we are doing what we love. In this day and time, one has to be wealthy in order to be able to do what they love.

A. What is Wealth?

Wealth is another way of saying "well-being". Our true wealth is our health. This is on all levels, spiritual, mental and physical. Spiritual health is the ability to see the why or purpose of things, mainly our own. Mental health is the ability to understand the how of things, or intelligence. Physical health is having all bodily functions operating optimally and able to perform physically without any hindrances. This comes from having the proper food, clothing, shelter, transportation and ability to rest and relax without working excessively. To achieve this balance in health one needs unlimited access to knowledge and resources. This equates to being rich by this world's standards. Lack in any area of our life will limit the level of happiness we experience. We need to be able to have all that we need to enjoy and experience and APPRECIATE every facet and activity of life that is in line with our positive growth and development. So in simple terms, it is necessary that we have enough money to secure all that is needed for us to unfold fully by developing all our faculties. This requires us having unrestricted access to anything we want. It takes the use and experiencing of things to fully develop all our faculties as well as express the ideas in us. We are happy most when we are able to give to those we love by way of guidance, inspiration, and pleasurable physical experiences.

Being rightly wealthy certainly produces happiness. Contrary to popular belief, one cannot be truly happy when they lack something they need or want in order to express what is in them. Poverty is a condition of lack of necessities therefore is certainly opposed to life and happiness. Everyone is wealthy by birthright. As Wallace D. Wattles eloquently explained in his classic book, The Science of Getting Rich, that our right to life is our right to having full access to everything needed for the full expression of all our talents and gifts. There is an abundant supply of everything needed for everyone to create their ideal life therefore no need for any of us to compete with one another. The thoughts we have come from an infinite source, and there is infinite energy to take the form of these thoughts. Everything we see in existence is energy that has taken the form of a particular thought. The

113

limitation to what we can create with our thoughts and experience in our lives is a result of our limited awareness of the possibilities that exist within us. The more aware we are, the more possibilities we realize therefore the more creative we become in shaping our reality to include all these possibilities. Everything we can ever think of is already here; we just have to become aware of it. We have to remember we are fractions and expressions of the Supreme Intelligence, the Creator, and the knowledge of the Creator is literally infinite. The inspirations we receive are in fact this supreme intelligence wanting to express itself through us. It would not attempt to express itself through a channel incapable of doing so. This means we are adequately equipped with the power within to realize any worthy goal to produce our dream reality that will add to life. Think of it this way, there was a time when horse and carriage was the most modern form of transportation. Then somebody became aware of the possibility of producing a horseless carriage, and went into motion to produce this reality. At first it was just a few vehicles that very few people even thought possible to own one. As more and more people became aware that they too can own a vehicle, means to produce them was furnished to those who stayed open to this possibility. Now we have millions and millions of vehicles on the road and many others in car sales parking lots and the capacity to produce many more. This shows us we have the capability to realize any dream we have. The limitation is what we impose on our own thinking by what we think is impossible. When we become aware that everything is possible, and everyone can actually live the life of their dream, the sooner we will literally have heaven on earth that all can enjoy. So lack and limitation are illusions we have to get out of our minds. This illusion of lack or scarcity has us competing with one another because we think there is a limited supply of opportunities and resources. We have to raise our awareness to the reality of infinite possibilities within and around us. We all can create what we want and actually have it, enjoy it and appreciate it, therefore becoming very happy. Imagine living the life of your dream, being healthy, intelligent, wealthy, having beautiful relationships, traveling anywhere you want to go, being able to give others as much as you want etc. How happy will you be?

B. Money

Money is a tool to manifest our ideas in an organized society. Money is energy and carries a vibration therefore only manifests in realities where there is a match in vibration. The thoughts we have control the vibration and frequency we carry. Having positive thoughts regarding money and what we can do with it will allow money to manifest in our reality. Money has the inherent nature to make people who possess it happy. Money is a reward we receive for services rendered. The more service we render the more money we receive. The more money we have, the more ability we have to acquire the things we need and want to fully express our gifts and talents. Bob Proctor, a great teacher on the wealth and prosperity mindset stated, and it is true, that money allows us to do basically two things; it makes us comfortable as well as allows us to extend our services beyond our immediate presence. When we are comfortable, we can be more creative. The more creative we are, the more good we add to the world. To generate money it is better to offer services that add to the life of the world while we spend our days doing what we love. This can be achieved by offering multiple services which produces multiple sources of income for us. In this manner we are multiplying our time through the efforts of others, versus trading our time for money working a job. The tendency to earn money through working a job, which the majority does, is not in our best interest, especially when the job is not something we are passionate about. It puts a limit to how much money we can earn because we all have a limited amount of time on the planet. We have to go into motion to see what type of services we can offer others that will make the world a better place and see ourselves getting abundantly rewarded for it financially. Money will allow us to receive everything we want to realize our ideal life and be of more service to humanity.

C. How to Acquire Wealth

We acquire wealth the right way by utilizing the creative process. This is when we employ our creativity to come up with the image of the wealth we want, what we are going to do with it and why. Then we put ourselves in harmony with the laws of nature that govern thought and motion. These are the laws that enable anything we think about to manifest in our reality. The purpose of our image is the fuel that will propel us to accomplish any goals we have in life. Purpose keeps us focused in all we do. An example of a purpose to one's life mission may be to ensure every person on the planet has unlimited access to clean water. So, all the goals one will set to accomplish in their life will be to serve that life purpose. The greater the purpose, the more drive and focus we have to realize it. In order to enjoy a life of peace, harmony, happiness and freedom, we have to make sure the purpose behind everything we think and do is aligned with the purpose of our very existence. Our purpose is to magnify or add to life. When anything we think and do is in opposition to the laws of nature, we pay for it through unnecessary pain and suffering. Even in our acquiring of wealth, it has to be done with a purpose to add to life. The wealth we get should be to allow us to serve others more.

We are to let our thoughts that we choose consciously control the results we get in our lives, instead of the common tendency to let our current results dictate to us the thoughts we have. The images we hold constantly in our minds determine the results we get. So when we focus on our current results, we are focusing on the same old image/thought, therefore we get more of the same. The solution is to observe the results and come up with different thoughts to produce different results and hold that image we want in our mind regardless of current appearances. Holding this image and experiencing this reality in our minds and EXPECTING to get it will motivate us to go into action and through that action we receive that reality in our physical world. This is how we consciously create the reality we want. Sounds simple right? The key is in DOING it. So let us have fun doing it!

D. Prayer

Most people are of the understanding that whatever you want to have or experience in your life, you have to pray for it. That is very true; however the concept of prayer has to be understood. We have to know and understand what prayer actually is, the proper way to pray and how prayer works. Prayer literally means practice. When we are praying for something, we are practicing the process of creating it. We are doing this by holding the image of the thing or experience we want in our life with unwavering faith that it will manifest and having deep gratitude for it as we would when we actually have it. This sets the creative forces in motion to bring to us what we want. Prayer is practicing moving a thought from the spiritual realm to its physical manifestation in our life. We are always praying or creating by the images we hold in our minds that consequently are manifesting as the results in our lives right now. It would be wise to practice holding and focusing on positive thoughts.

We should focus our attention on things we want to do, have and be because that is what we will attract into our lives. When we focus on things we don't like, that is the image we are holding and praying for and we will inevitably attract it into our life experience. Thoughts are processed as images in our minds, these images generate feelings, these feelings motivate us to act, and our actions produce our results, good or bad. We are the architects of our reality, not someone or something outside of us. So, let us practice thinking about or holding the images of what we want, be it health, wealth, relationships, happiness, prosperity etc. We reap what we sow. We get back what we send out. We attract what we expect. Expect only good things and be grateful for them. The more we express gratitude for what we have, even just in our imagination, the more we will receive to be grateful for.

To have the right vibration to attract wealth and be free and happy, let us remember these keys:

- Everything is energy and a manifestation of thought
- We are thought evolved beings with creative abilities
- We create our reality by the images we constantly hold in our minds
- We have the power to create anything we want in our minds and bring it into our world through living by the law, therefore we are not in competition with anyone
- There is no lack of opportunity or resources for everyone to create the life they want
- We have to focus our attention on the reality we want regardless of current results
- To be wealthy we have to think and see ourselves wealthy

- We are to be grateful for everything in the image of what we want just as we would when we receive it
- To receive what we want we have to stay in motion performing positive deeds with unwavering faith that what we want is already coming to us and be grateful for it
- The more grateful we are for what we have the more we will receive to be grateful for
- Our right to life is our right to having all the money we need to acquire everything we need and want to fully express all the talents and gifts within us
- Money is a tool to assist us with acquiring everything we need to manifest ideas
- Money will enable us to be comfortable and extend our services beyond our immediate presence
- Money is a reward for service rendered, so more service equals more money
- We are to offer service that makes the world a better place by adding to life
- We are to spend our days doing what we love and completing every task successfully because every success opens the way for more success
- The wealthy lifestyle we seek will come to us by way of the established channels of trade and commerce and we have to stay active to receive it
- Constant contemplation of the image of the wealth we want with steady faith in its realization while being deeply grateful for having received it will speed up its physical manifestation in our life

Personal Experiences

One thing I have come to understand through my experiences is how all knowledge and wisdom I have gained should be applied in such a way as to make me a more efficient and productive person. I am most efficient when it takes me minimal time and effort to get a goal completed and most productive when I manage to achieve what I set out to do. Whenever I accomplish tasks on my to-do list, that shows me the progress I am making towards reaching my goals. Since I have been applying the ideas in this book to my own thinking and motion, I have witnessed great improvements in my health, clarity of thought, more control of my emotions and peace of mind.

Another area of my life that showcases the tremendous benefits of positive living is my family. I have a wonderful wife and three beautiful children that are happy, healthy, and civilized. My wife and I consistently teach our children to respect peace, order, harmony and life. They know to say excuse me when they unintentionally make a loud sound that breaks the peace. One example is when we visited my wife's aunt and my then 5 year-old son unintentionally slammed the door leaving the house and then came back and said excuse me and proceeded to gently close the door quietly. My wife's aunt was amazed at the level of awareness to peace and order my son displayed. She still talks to other people about how wonderful and well-behaved our children are. As parents, we apply the principles of speaking to our children in a way that ensures they know that they can do anything they put their mind to and can have anything they want that is of right. They know the importance of checking and never assuming. They know what expressions are negative like frowning, wearing a gloomy face, and bad attitudes so much so they make it a point to point it out when they see characters or people in movies or video games expressing negative. We keep them from violent and meaningless activities that do not develop them into positive adults. They rarely watch any TV. We have no TV service in the house. We utilize the internet to connect with the outside world as far as current events are concerned. We monitor everything they eat, read and listen to so they are exposed to what is beneficial to them. I encourage them to stay in touch with nature by playing outdoors and respecting animals and plants the way they are to be respected.

To ensure our home is as hygienic as possible, we ask everyone, to remove their shoes at the door so that no dirt from outside is brought into the house. Many people are uncomfortable asking people to take their shoes off in their homes because do not want to inconvenience their guests. Some have no problem with people wearing shoes from outside inside the house, yet they will throw a fit if somebody brought a pinch of dirt from outside and sprinkled it throughout the house. The same thing or worse is happening when one walks in the house with their shoes from outside. If one respects life and health, they should easily see the wisdom in that practice and should promptly adopt it for their own home.

Conclusion

The ideas covered in this book are a blueprint to the science of living. Understanding what life is, how it came about, its purpose, our part in it and how to accurately perform our part is indeed the awareness that all intelligent beings need in order to live life fully. The ability to live life as it was designed without any restrictions is freedom. This book inspires, motivates and empowers one who applies the ideas in it to experience the life of their dreams in joy, peace and freedom. Now that we know how to find and fulfill our purpose in the world freely, the only thing between us and our dreams is now our willingness to attain them. Where there is a will there is a way. The more willing we are, the clearer the path to attaining what we want. Below is a summary of the fundamental ideas discussed in this book that are the keys to living a life of purpose, happiness and freedom.

Life is intelligent motion that inspires us to enjoy the present with high anticipation of the future. It takes awareness to experience life and it can only be experienced properly when we are doing what we love. Everything is energy and all is a manifestation of thought; energy with direction. There are two forces in creation, positive and negative, in constant battle for singularity. Positive is the generator of constructive ideas that produce intelligent motion and negative is the reactionary destructive force that is opposed to life. These two forces are the reason for the two opposing natures in us; one inspires us to dream and attain high goals in order to fully experience life while the other discourages us and influences us to do things that are against our very own creativity and existence. All that exists is an expression of either of these forces. We are expressing one of these forces in all we think and do, and there is no in-between. As we think, we are either expressing the Positive/Right, or the opposite, which is negative/wrong. There is no YOU or ME in between, just those two forces. All wisdom is geared to inspire us to express Positive and be an addition to life and peace. When we think and perform positive deeds, we are expressing the fraction of the Creator, which is who we are at our very essence and the entire Creation comes to our aid in all we do. The ability to think factually is the key to discerning positive from negative and ensuring we are able to accomplish our positive ideas absent of the negative influences. To assist with strengthening the positive side of us and checking the negative nature in us, proper diet is essential. Since we are what we think, it is important for us to practice looking at life positively so that we can only attract and manifest positive circumstances and experiences in our life. As unique individuals it is important for us to know what we love doing that makes us happy and adds to life and peace and have faith in our ability to do, have and become what we want as that is our unique purpose. To achieve what we want, we have to practice imagining ourselves already experiencing it. We should also know, without a doubt, that we will receive that reality and be as grateful for it in our imagination as we will when we have it physically and then set goals to achieve. This process will take us to where we want to be in life. Successful accomplishment of these goals will require exercising self-discipline, focus, persistence and many other positive habits already outlined in the book.

We have covered in detail what freedom is, how to attain it and how to perpetuate it on all three levels of existence, spiritual, mental and physical. YOU are here on the planet to achieve something only you can do. What is it that you really want to do with your life? What legacy do you want to leave in the world? You have the tools to do, have and become anything you want in this book. Diligently study and apply them to become the successful and free human being you were put on this planet to be.

In closing let us remember these key points and keep them at the forefront of our minds:

- Freedom is that which is absent of opposition. It is the ability to express life, or intelligent motion, in its purity.
- Freedom can only be achieved when one is in harmony with the laws of creation or nature, by thinking and doing right.
- Right is that which can be proven and is in agreement with nature and promotes Life and peace.
- Freedom can only be realized outside when it exists inside, in our minds.
- The more one grows and develops in awareness, the more freedom they are capable of experiencing.
- The amount of truth or right one applies in their life equals the degree of freedom one experiences.

Remember to share the insights you have now gained from reading this book with others. The more people you have around you that know what you now know, the easier it will be to keep growing because you then have others to support you. Also as you share these ideas with others, it helps with clarifying them in your own mind as well as making them a part of yourself, or your everyday thinking.

Go ahead and live the life you were designed to live, in peace, love, harmony and freedom!

About Me (the Author)

I was born in Zimbabwe, where I grew up until I was 23. In my search for satisfaction and fulfillment, I decided to leave and study overseas in the USA, and this is where I am residing at the time of this writing.

Growing up, I was always in a group setting, which taught me how to be tactful and considerate of others. I came from a big family, and grew up enjoying both urban and rural life. My family implemented both traditional and Christian lifestyles. I attended boarding school for the last 6 of my 13 years of organized schooling. In high school I always studied subjects of interest about how things worked. Things like cars, planes, TVs, steam engines etc. I would be excited to teach others what I learned so that I could have others to discuss what I know with. It perplexed me why we were only studying fragments of certain subjects like physics, biology, chemistry etc. when there were many more fascinating things to learn that would make our understanding of the subject complete. I saw that with a more complete understanding we could do something meaningful with the knowledge, like inventions that improve life for all.

After focusing on computer studies in the last 2 years of high school, I naturally gravitated towards the IT industry for career options and secured a job as a computer technician. I learned hands-on how to setup, maintain and fix computer systems and networks. As I grew in my understanding of this field of work through individual studying and experimenting, the respect I received from others around also improved. This made me aware that if I want to rise rank in society or progress in life, I have to be willing to reach out for knowledge on my own and experiment with it to gain mastery. This would increase my power of influence on my environment and my living conditions. The more ideas I gained mastery over, the more my skills became highly sought after, which increased my self-worth. I was getting paid generously; however because of lack of direction in my life, I partied a lot as a way to find fulfillment. I blamed everything and everybody else for things that were not working in my life. My rebellious attitude towards life led me to drink excessively as well as making unintelligent decisions. Some of which almost cost me my life on multiple occasions. I intuitively knew there was a better way to live my life however did not know how to go about it.

My inspiration to start seeking Truth came from my constant yearning to understand life better; I wanted to grasp the system that governs everything that happens with us. I wanted to know the meaning of it all, especially the injustices, and why there were so many disparities in the living conditions of people on the same planet who seem to have the same capabilities. Since childhood I had always wondered why there was such an unfair distribution of wealth, and as I grew older, the question was getting faint. When I moved from Zimbabwe and came to the USA in 2000 and started witnessing the miserable condition some people were in, the question got re-ignited. This time it sparked even more questions like how is it that such a "rich and developed" country was neglecting its own citizens by leaving them to wallow in poverty yet others were extremely rich? What set of morals were the ruling class operating on? Who was going to correct all these injustices so that everyone can enjoy life equally? These questions came and went. My associates and I debated about these issues without ever coming to a definite conclusion. We would discuss politics as if that was the main cause of the suffering of people. One thing we always agreed on is that things could be better and a change was needed.

When my mother passed away in 2002, I found myself wanting to know more about Life, like where exactly did we come from and where do we go when we pass on? I asked many of the people I knew and nobody had an answer. Some even discouraged me to think about it too much and some flat out said nobody knows. Those responses sounded absurd to me. My yearning for an answer just intensified. For the first time I realized that most people had no clue what life was about and I would be a fool to rely on them to get a better understanding of life. I made a decision to find out because I figured somebody somewhere knows the answer. I reasoned that since we were created by somebody or something, then it would make sense that true knowledge about life was passed down from the first man created down to this present generation.

One day while at work, a colleague I was studying with ran into a website of a community rebuilding program in Kansas City, KS that was teaching formulas of accurate thinking in order to produce tangible solutions to everyday problems.

The program's focus was on personal and community development, so there were experts in different fields that came and shared their knowledge which added to the awareness of those in the program. The main focus in everything we learned was the proper way to think, holistic health and civilization (how to treat everything and everyone right). Some of the most profound books I came across while in the program were "As a Man Thinketh" by James Allen and "The Kybalion" by the Three Initiates. We also focused on learning to identify the pattern of life in everything by asking the question WHY until there is no more WHY to ask. And as you might have noticed with this book, one of the foundational teachings was on the reality of the Positive and Negative forces and how they operate within us and how to use this knowledge to stay positive and be successful in everything we do. Also, of importance in the program was the production and promotion of functional family units that raised healthy, intelligent and productive children.

What I learned has enabled me and my wife to start a family, produce healthy and positively intelligent children. We have weathered problems and misunderstandings by addressing them intelligently and putting peaceful resolutions in place instead of trying to win arguments like most people do. We still encounter issues on certain things as we grow closer together however we know we will always come out victorious and wiser when we apply the formulas of proper thinking in our interactions. We focus on what is right instead of who is right and that approach seems to work all the time.

I consider myself a thought evolved being, a being of intelligence, so with that, I do not subscribe to one school of thought because all schools of thought are branches trying to explain the same thing, Life/Creation/Nature/Universe/God/Jehovah/Allah etc. I accept and acknowledge truth from everything and everyone, therefore I am widely read. I have read different scriptures, mainly the Bible, and extracted the truth in them that applied to my life situation and almost every day I am learning one more simple truth to add to what I already knew. So the perspective I am coming from in this book is from a human being interested in understanding life better so that I can express the ideas in me more to serve others better. And because I understand we are all fractions of one WHOLE, when I share what I have learned that I know works, because I tried it myself, I am empowering others, which in turn empowers me too as more and more people awaken to their infinite power and start expressing it to make the world a better place for all. My targeted audience is those people who know there is a better way to live their life however don't know how to do it, and even more so those who think they have everything in life figured out, because there is a very important thought process that my book delivers or installs into their thinking that will make them much more effective and successful in everything they do. The proper understanding of the concept of the Positive and Negative forces and how to utilize factual thinking to stay focused on the Positive is the key that has been missing almost in all of creation until now. This is why advanced civilizations and nations have always risen and then fell, because its rulers and citizens succumbed to this negative force.

The truth about life and what makes it work right has freed me from living in darkness. KNOWING who I am and my purpose on the planet, which consequently freed me from ignorance, fear, doubt and disbelief in my own abilities to produce the life that I want to see and experience. Operating in darkness produces all the negatives like despair, disappointment, stress, disease etc. Now that I am operating from the light, which keeps getting brighter, the negative expressions are vanishing from my reality in proportion to the brightness of my light. Since I know that I am the master of my destiny, captain of my ship and architect of my reality, I also know that there is no limit to what I can achieve. This new awareness has given me a peace of mind like no other, and it keeps getting better every day as my understanding of life deepens. For example, one of my goals in life is to become a world class author and life coach. That goal is actually manifesting in degrees, just as everything else in nature grows gradually to give everything else around it time to adjust. This first book I have produced and everything it has already started doing for and in me is propelling me to the realization of my dream, which is the life of a highly sought after author and life instructor, among other things. All the feedback I am getting from my writings is enabling me to readjust my message to make it more effective. After doing these readjustments and revisions a number of times, what will result is one of the most effective personal and community development curriculums on the planet.

My life is a clear demonstration of the laws of nature at work, primarily because I set out to find a solution to the world's problems, and though it took me almost a decade, I can safely and confidently say I found the answer. And most importantly, I also gained the understanding of the solution by applying it and seeing tangible results in my life. The first step after learning and mastering something is to teach it to others. This is where I am now. My mission is to continue learning about life and then teaching others so that we can grow together into being truly free.

When I started the process of waking up through studying myself, or looking within, I started participating in many online forums where I was always sharing the wonderful ideas about life I had become aware of, thinking many other people would be excited to hear it too as to answer those questions in their heads that I know they had because

I had them too. I know I tried to silence them however that did not work. I understood all the partying in the world will not bring me the fulfillment I was yearning for. This process of online interactions helped clarify things in my own head as I shared ideas that make life work right with others. With the advent of Facebook, I was able to connect and share my new understanding of life with others, which caused me to learn quickly that when I stand up for the truth, I should be prepared to stand alone.

After helping answer numerous questions which brought peace of mind to others, I started seeing the possibility of me putting a book together of compiled online discussions. I reasoned if one person is gaining something, many others might also benefit. Other people I was in communication with also recommended I write a book, so I started giving it serious thought. It provided a way for me to help spread positive ideas so that others can start experiencing more and more positives, like good health, high spirits, harmonious relationships, peace of mind and success in all they do.

So, this book is my first attempt to utilize mass media to project and spread light and love into the world. I have put together ideas that give more insight into one of the subjects I enjoy talking about with others most because of the power I see coming from it the more it is understood. That idea is FREEDOM. This idea encapsulates the essence of Life. Understanding it equals understanding Life and its purpose. This book is my way of reaching out to those in the same situation I was in, of wanting to understand life better and know for certainty how to live it the way it was designed to be lived. There are many other ideas that have to be gone into in detail however the schematic of Life is clearly explained in this book. With this book, you now have more options so that you are never at the mercy of something opposed to your survival.

I will that the ideas in this book benefit you as much as they have and are benefiting me and my family.

I am eternally grateful for all the wonderful teachers out there who have shared with me pieces of themselves to make me who and what I am in this present moment.

Thank you.

Livingstone Bvumbi

www.ingramcontent.com/pod-product-compliance
Lightning Source LLC
Chambersburg PA
CBHW071556040426
42452CB00008B/1187